THE HISTORICAL NOVEL
AND OTHER ESSAYS

THE
HISTORICAL NOVEL
AND OTHER ESSAYS

BY

BRANDER MATTHEWS

Essay Index Reprint Series

BOOKS FOR LIBRARIES PRESS

FREEPORT, NEW YORK

First published 1901
Reprinted 1968

809
M 42 h
65518
April 1969

LIBRARY OF CONGRESS CATALOG CARD NUMBER:
68-20320

TO

MARK TWAIN

IN TESTIMONY OF MY REGARD FOR THE MAN
AND OF MY RESPECT FOR THE
LITERARY ARTIST

CONTENTS

I

THE HISTORICAL NOVEL

THE HISTORICAL NOVEL

WHEN Robert Louis Stevenson wrote his 'Note on Realism,' and declared that "the historical novel is dead," he did not think he would live to be the author of the 'Master of Ballantrae.' But when Prosper Mérimée expressed to a correspondent his belief that the historical novel was a "bastard form," he could look back without reproach upon his own 'Chronique de Charles IX' — one of the finest examples of the kind of fiction he chose to despise. Whether or not most readers of English fiction at the end of the nineteenth century approve Mérimée's opinion that the historical novel is illegitimate by birth, few of them will agree with Stevenson in deeming it defunct. If we can judge by the welcome it receives from the writers of newspaper notices, it is not moribund even; and if we are influenced by the immense sale of 'Ben-Hur' and by the broadening vogue of 'Quo Vadis,' we may go so far as to believe that it was never stronger or fuller of life.

We might even suggest that the liking for historical fiction is now so keen that the public is not at all particular as to the veracity of the history out of which the fiction has been manufactured, since it accepts the invented facts of the Chronicles of Zenda quite as eagerly as it receives the better-documented 'Memoirs of a Minister of France.'

More than any other British author of his years, Stevenson worked in accord with the theories of art which have been elaborated and expounded in France; and it may be that when he declared the historical novel to be dead he was thinking rather of French literature than of English. There is no doubt that in France the historical novel is not cherished. No one of the living masters of fiction in France has attempted any but contemporary studies. M. Daudet, M. Zola, M. Bourget, find all the subjects they need in the life of their own times. Flaubert's fame is due to his masterly 'Madame Bovary,' and not to his splendid 'Salammbô.' So sharp is the French reaction against Romanticism that even impressionist critics like M. Jules Lemaître and M. Anatole France do not overpraise the gay romances of the elder Dumas, as Stevenson did. In France the historical novel has no standing in the court of serious criticism. As Mérimée wrote in the correspondence from which one quotation has

4

already been made, "History, in my eyes, is a sacred thing."

Historical fiction suffers in France from the same discredit as historical painting, and for the same reasons. It is either too easy to be worth while — a French critic might say — or so difficult as to be impossible. When a young man once went to Courbet for advice, saying that his vocation was to be a historical painter, the artist promptly responded: "I don't doubt it; and therefore begin by giving three months to making a portrait of your father!"

Perhaps French opinion is nowhere more accurately voiced than by M. Anatole France in the 'Jardin d'Épicure': "We cannot reproduce with any accuracy what no longer exists. When we see that a painter has to take all the trouble in the world to represent to us, more or less exactly, a scene in the time of Louis Philippe, we may despair of his ever being able to give us the slightest idea of an event contemporary with Saint Louis or Augustus. We weary ourselves copying armor and old chests; but the artists of the past did not worry themselves about so empty an exactness. They lent to the hero of legend or history the costume and the looks of their own contemporaries; and thus they depicted naturally their own soul and their own century. Now what can an artist do better?"

5

In other words, Paul Veronese's 'Marriage at Cana' is frankly a revelation of the Italian Renascence; and this revelation is not contaminated by any fifteenth-century guess at the manners and customs of Judea in the first century. It is difficult to surmise how some of the laboriously archeological pictures of the nineteenth century will affect an observer of the twenty-first century. As in painting, so in the drama: Shakspere made no effort to suggest the primitive manners and customs of Scotland to the spectators of his 'Macbeth'; and if the characters of 'Julius Cæsar' are Roman, it is chiefly because of the local color that chanced to leak through from North's Plutarch. What Shakspere aimed at was the creation of living men and women — interesting because of their intense humanity, eternal because of their truth and vitality. He never sought to differentiate Scotchmen and Danes of the past from Englishmen of the present. He lent to all his personages the vocabulary, the laws, the usages, the costumes which were familiar to the playgoers that flocked to applaud his pieces. Archeology was unknown to him and to them; anachronism did not affright them or him. Probably he would have brushed aside any demand for exactness of fact as an attempt to impose an unfair restraint upon the liberty of the dramatist — whose business it was to write plays to be acted in a theater, and not to prepare lectures to be delivered in a college hall. Shakspere and Veronese, each in his own art, worked freely, as though wholly unconscious of any difference between their own contemporaries and the subjects of the Cæsars.

The compilers of the ' Gesta Romanorum ' had no conception of the elements of either geography or chronology; and the authors of the Romances of Chivalry seem to have been as ignorant, although their scientific nihilism is perhaps wilful — like Stockton's when he tells us a ' Tale of Negative Gravity.' The essential likeness of the Romances of Chivalry to the Waverley Novels has been pointed out more than once; and in each group of tales we find the hero, or the technical hero's rescuing friend, omnipresent, omniscient, and almost omnipotent. The essential difference between the two kinds of fiction is quite as obvious also: it lies in the fact that Scott and his followers know what history is, and that even when they vary from it they are aware of what they are doing.

The historical novel, as we understand it today, like the historical drama and like historical painting, could not come into being until after history had established itself, and after chronology and geography had lent to history their indispensable aid. Nowadays the novelist and the drama-

7

tist and the painter are conscious that people do not talk and dress and behave as they did a hundred years ago, or a thousand. They do not know precisely how the people of those days did feel and think and act: they cannot know these things. The most they can do is to study the records of the past and make a guess, the success of which depends on their equipment and insight. They accept their obligation to history and to its handmaids — an obligation which Shakspere and Veronese would have denied quite as frankly as the compilers of the 'Gesta Romanorum' or the writers of the Romances of Chivalry. Scott was appealing to a circle of more or less sophisticated readers, any one of whom might be an antiquary: he was to be tried by a jury of his peers. But the author of 'Amadis of Gaul,' for example, wrote for a public that cared as little as he himself did about the actual facts of the countries or of the periods his hero traversed in search of strange adventure.

Although it is not difficult to detect here and there in Scott's predecessors the more or less fragmentary hints of which he availed himself, it would be absurd to deny that Scott is really the inventor of the historical novel, just as Poe was afterward the inventor of the detective story. In the 'Castle of Otranto' Horace Walpole essayed to recall to life the Gothic period as he understood it; but — if we may judge by Mrs. Radcliffe and the rest of his immediate imitators — it was the tale of mystery he succeeded in writing and not the true historical novel. For this last, Walpole was without two things which Scott possessed abundantly — the gift of story-telling and an intimate knowledge of more than one epoch of the past.

And Scott had also two other qualifications which Walpole lacked: he was a poet and he was a humorist. As it happens, the steps that led Scott to the Waverley Novels are not hard to count. He began by collecting the ballads of the Border; and soon he wrote new ballads in the old manner. Then he linked ballads together, and so made 'Marmion' and the 'Lady of the Lake.' When he thought that the public was weary of his verse, he told one of these ballad tales in prose, and so made 'Waverley.' But he had read Miss Edgeworth, and he wished to do for the Scottish peasant what she had done for the Irish: thus it is that the prose tales contained sketches of character at once robust and delicate. In time, when he tired of Scotch subjects, he crossed the Border; and in 'Ivanhoe' he first applied to an English subject the formula he had invented for use in North Britain, helped in his handling of a medieval theme by his recollections of the 'Götz von Berlichingen' of Goethe, which he had translated in his prentice days. After a while he crossed the Channel, and found that the method acquired in telling the Scotch stories enabled him to write 'Quentin Durward,' a story of France, and the 'Talisman,' a story of Palestine. Although he had to forego his main advantage when he left his native land, Scott did not abandon his humor; and these later tales contain more than one memorable character, even if they reveal none so unforgetable as are a dozen or more in the Scotch stories.

Probably the immense vogue of the Waverley Novels, as they came forth swiftly one after another in the first quarter of the nineteenth century, was due rather to the qualities they had in common with the 'Castle of Otranto' than to the qualities they had in common with 'Castle Rackrent.' No doubt it was the union of the merits of both schools that broadened the audience to which the Waverley Novels appealed; but, in attaining his contemporary triumph, Scott owed more to Horace Walpole than to Maria Edgeworth. He surpassed Walpole immeasurably, because he was a man of deeper knowledge and broader sympathy. His audience was far wider than Miss Edgeworth's, because he infused into his Scottish tales a romantic flavor which she carefully excluded from her veracious portrayals of Irish character.

Yet it may be suggested that the stories of Scott most likely to survive the centenary of their publication and to retain readers in the first quarter of the twentieth century are perhaps those in which he best withstands the comparison with Miss Edgeworth — the stories in which he has recorded types of Scottish character, with its mingled humor and pathos. For mere excitement our liking is eternal: but the fashion thereof is fickle; and we prefer our romantic adventures cut this way to-day and another way to-morrow. Our interest in our fellow-man subsists unchanged forever, and we take a perennial delight in the revelation of the subtleties of human nature. It is in the 'Antiquary' and in the 'Heart of Midlothian' that Scott is seen at his best; and it is by creating characters like Caleb Balderstone and Dugald Dalgetty and Wandering Willie that he has deserved to endure.

In work of this kind Scott showed himself a Realist. He revealed himself as a humorist with a compassionate understanding of his fellow-creatures. He gave play to that sense of reality which Bagehot praises as one of the most valuable of his characteristics. When he is dealing with medieval life, — which he knew not at first hand, as he knew his Scottish peasants, but afar off from books, — the result is unreal. He was as well read in history as any man of his time; and he

himself explained his superiority over the host of
imitators who encompassed him about, by saying that they read to write, while he wrote
because he had read. But this knowledge was
second-hand, at best: it was not like his day-in-
day-out acquaintance with the men of his own
time; and this is why the unreality of 'Ivanhoe,'
for instance, is becoming more and more obvious
to us. The breaking of the lances in the lists of
Ashby-de-la-Zouch is to us a hollow sham, like
the polite tournament at Eglinton. The deeds
of daring of Ivanhoe and of the Black Knight and
of Robin Hood still appeal to the boy in us; but
they are less and less convincing to the man.

Although Ivanhoe and Robin Hood and the
Black Knight are boldly projected figures, their
psychology is summary. How could it be anything else? With all his genius, Scott was emphatically a man of his own time and of his
own country, with the limitations and the prejudices of the eighteenth century and of the British
Isles. Few of his warmest admirers would venture to suggest that he was as broad in sympathy
as Shakspere, or as universal in his vision; and
yet he was trying to reconstruct the past for us,
in deed and feeling and thought—the very thing
that Shakspere never attempted. The author of
'Much Ado about Nothing' and of the 'Comedy
of Errors' was content to people the foreign plots

he borrowed so lightly with the Elizabethans he knew so well. The author of 'Ivanhoe' and of the 'Talisman' made a strenuous effort to body forth the very spirit of epochs and of lands wholly unlike the spirit of the eighteenth century in the British Isles. It is a proof of Scott's genius that he came so near success; but failure was inevitable. "After all," said Taine, "his characters, to whatever age he transports them, are his neighbors—canny farmers, vain lairds, gloved gentlemen, young marriageable ladies, all more or less commonplace, that is, well ordered by education and character, hundreds of miles away from the voluptuous fools of the Restoration or the heroic brutes and forcible beasts of the Middle Ages."

The fact is that no man can step off his own shadow. By no effort of the will can he thrust himself backward into the past and shed his share of the accumulations of the ages, of all the myriad accretions of thought and sentiment and knowledge, stored up in the centuries that lie between him and the time he is trying to treat. Of necessity he puts into his picture of days gone by more or less of the days in which he is living. Shakspere frankly accepted the situation: Scott attempted the impossible. Racine wrote tragedies on Greek subjects; and he submitted to be bound by rules which he supposed to have been laid down by a great Greek critic. To the spectator who saw these plays when they were first produced, they may have seemed Greek; but to us, two hundred years later, they appear to be perhaps the most typical product of the age of Louis XIV; and a great French critic has suggested that to bring out their full flavor they should be performed nowadays by actors wearing, not the flowing draperies of Athens, but the elaborate court-dress of Versailles. 'Phèdre' is interesting to us to-day, not because it is Greek, but because it is French; and some of Scott's stories, hailed on their publication as faithful reproductions of medieval manners, will doubtless have another interest, in time, as illustrations of what the beginning of the nineteenth century believed the Middle Ages to be.

Not only is it impossible for a man to get away from his own country, but it is equally impossible for him to get away from his own nationality. How rarely has an author been able to create a character of a different stock from his own! Certainly most of the great figures of fiction are compatriots of their makers. We have had many carpet-bag novelists of late — men and women who go forth gaily and study a foreign country from the platform of a parlor-car; and some of these are able to spin yarns which hold the attention of listening thousands. What the people of the foreign countries think of these superficial tales we can measure when we recall the contempt in which we Americans hold the efforts made by one and another of the British novelists to lay the scene of a story here in the United States. Dickens and Trollope and Reade were men of varied gifts, keen observers all of them; but how lamentable the spectacle when they endeavored to portray an American! Probably most American endeavors to portray an Englishman are quite as foolish in the eyes of the British. Dickens twice chose to compete with the carpet-bag novelists; and if we Americans are unwilling to see a correct picture of our life in 'Martin Chuzzlewit,' we may be sure that the French are as unwilling to acknowledge the 'Tale of Two Cities' as an accurate portrayal of the most dramatic epoch in their history. There are those who think it was a piece of impertinence for a Londoner like Dickens to suppose that he could escape the inexorable limitations of his birth and education and hope to see Americans or Frenchmen as they really are; finer artists than Dickens have failed in this — artists of a far more exquisite touch.

The masterpieces of the great painters instantly declare the race to which the limner himself belonged. Rubens and Velasquez and Titian traveled and saw the world; they have left us portraits of men of many nationalities: and yet every man and woman Rubens painted seems to us Dutch; every man and woman Velasquez painted seems to us Spanish; every man and woman Titian painted seems to us Italian. The artists of our own time, for all their cosmopolitanism, are no better off; and when M. Bonnat has for sitters Americans of marked characteristics he cannot help reproducing them on canvas as though they had been reflected in a Gallic mirror. In short, a man can no more escape from his race than he can escape from his century; it is the misfortune of the historical novelist that he must try to do both.

The 'Atalanta in Calydon' of Mr. Swinburne has been praised as the most Greek of all modern attempts to reproduce Greek tragedy; and it may deserve this eulogy — but what of it? It may be the most Greek of the modern plays, but is it really Greek after all? Would not an ancient Greek have found in it many things quite incomprehensible to him? Even if it is more or less Greek, is it as Greek as the plays the Greeks themselves wrote? Why should an Englishman pride himself on having written a Greek play? At best he has but accomplished a feat of main strength, a *tour de force*, an exercise in literary gymnastics! A *pastiche*, a paste jewel, is not a precious possession. A Greek play written by a modern Englishman remains absolutely outside the current of contemporary literature. It is a kind of thing the Greeks never dreamed of doing; they wrote Greek plays because they were Greeks and could do nothing else; they did not imitate the literature of the Assyrians nor that of the Egyptians; they swam in the full center of the current of their own time. If Sophocles were a modern Englishman, who can doubt that he would write English plays, with no backward glance toward Greek tragedy? The lucidity, the sobriety, the elevation of the Greeks we may borrow from them, if we can, without taking over also the mere external forms due to the accidents of their age.

Art has difficulties enough without imposing on it limitations no longer needful. Let the dead past bury its dead. This has been the motto of every great artist, ancient and modern, of Dante, of Shakspere, and of Molière. A man who has work to do in the world does not embarrass himself by using a dead language to convey his ideas. Milton's Latin verse may be as elegant as its admirers assert; but if he had written nothing else, this page might need a foot-note to explain who he was. If a layman may venture an opinion, the use of Gothic architecture in America at the end of the nineteenth century seems an equivalent anachronism. Gothic is a dead language; and no man to-day in the

United States uses it naturally, as he does the vernacular. One of the most accomplished of American architects recently drew attention to the fact that "such a perfect composition and exquisite design as M. Vaudremer's church of Montrouge, Paris, unquestionably the best and ablest attempt in our time to revive medieval art, is considered cold even by his own pupils"; and then Mr. Hastings explains that "this is because it lacks the life we are living, and at the same time is without the real medieval life." Gothic was at its finest when it was the only architecture that was known, and when it was used naturally and handled freely and unconsciously — just as the best Greek plays were written by the Greeks.

In other words, the really trustworthy historical novels are those which were a-writing while the history was a-making. If the 'Tale of Two Cities' misrepresents the Paris of 1789, the 'Pickwick Papers' represents with amazing humor and with photographic fidelity certain aspects of the London of 1837. The one gives us what Dickens guessed about France in the preceding century, and the other tells us what he saw in England in his own time. Historical novel for historical novel, 'Pickwick' is superior to the 'Tale of Two Cities,' and 'Nicholas Nickleby' to 'Barnaby Rudge.' No historical novelist will

ever be able to set before us the state of affairs in
the South in the decade preceding the Civil War
with the variety and the veracity of 'Uncle Tom's
Cabin,' written in that decade. No American
historian has a more minute acquaintance with
the men who made the United States than Mr.
Paul Leicester Ford; and yet one may venture to
predict that Mr. Ford will never write a historical
novel having a tithe of the historical value possessed by his suggestive study of the conditions
of contemporary politics in New York city, the
'Honorable Peter Stirling.' Nevertheless there
are few librarians bold enough to catalogue 'Pickwick' and 'Uncle Tom' and 'Peter Stirling' under
historical fiction.

One of the foremost merits of the novel, as of
the drama, is that it enlarges our sympathy. It
compels us to shift our point of view, and often
to assume that antithetic to our custom. It forces
us to see not only how the other half lives, but
also how it feels and how it thinks. We learn
not merely what the author meant to teach us:
we absorb, in addition, a host of things he did
not know he was putting in — things he took
for granted, some of them, and things he implied
as a matter of course. This unconscious richness of instruction cannot but be absent from
the historical novel — or at best it is so obscured
as to be almost non-existent.

In 'Anna Karénina' one can see Russian life in the end of this century as Tolstoy knows it, having beheld it with his own eyes: in 'War and Peace' we have Russian life in the beginning of this century as Tolstoy supposes it to have been, not having seen it. One is the testimony of an eye-witness: the other is given on information and belief. 'Pendennis' and the 'Newcomes' and 'Vanity Fair'—for all that the last includes the battle of Waterloo, fought when Thackeray was but a boy—are written out of the fulness of knowledge: 'Henry Esmond' is written out of the fulness of learning only. In the former there is an unconscious accuracy of reproduction, while in the latter unconsciousness is impossible. The historical novel cannot help being what the French call *voulu*—a word that denotes both effort and artificiality. The story-teller who deals honestly with his own time achieves, without taking thought, a fidelity simply impossible to the story-teller who deals with the past, no matter how laboriously the latter may toil after it.

In fact, the more he labors, the less life is there likely to be in the tale he is telling: humanity is choked by archeology. It calls for no research to set forth the unending conflict of duty and desire, for example. If we examine carefully the best of the stories usually classed under historical

fiction we shall find those to be the most satisfactory in which the history is of least importance,
in which it is present only as a background.
The examination may lead to a subdivision of
the class of historical fiction into the actual historical novel and the novel in which history is
wholly subordinate, not to say merely incidental.
A British critic, Professor George Saintsbury,
has laid down the law that "the true historical
novelist employs the reader's presumed interest
in historical scene and character as an instrument
to make his own work attractive." Although it
would be easy to dissent from this dictum, it may
be used to explain the distinction drawn in the
preceding paragraph. A tale of the past is not
necessarily a true historical novel: it is a true historical novel only when the historical events are
woven into the texture of the story. Applying
this test, we see that the 'Bride of Lammermoor'
is not a true historical novel; and this is perhaps
the reason why it is held in high esteem by all
lovers of genuine Romance. By the same token,
the 'Scarlet Letter' is not a true historical novel.

Neither in the 'Bride of Lammermoor' nor in
the 'Scarlet Letter' is there any reliance upon
historical scene or character for attraction. Scott
was narrating again a legend of an inexplicable
mystery: but although the period of its occur-
rence was long past when he wrote, he presented

simply the characters enmeshed in the fateful adventure, and relied for the attractiveness of his story upon the inherent interest of the weird climax toward which the reader is hurried breathless under the weight of impending doom. Hawthorne was captivated by a study of conscience, the incidents of which could be brought out more conveniently and more effectively by throwing back the time of the tale into the remote past.

In another story of Scott's, not equal to the 'Bride of Lammermoor' in its tragic intensity, but superb in its resolute handling of emotion, the 'Heart of Midlothian,' there is perhaps a stiffer infusion of actual history; but it would be rash to suggest that in its composition the author relied on historical scene or character to make his work attractive. The attraction of the 'Heart of Midlothian' lies in its presentation of character at the crisis of its existence. So in the 'Romola' of George Eliot, although the author obviously spent her strength in trying to transmute the annals of Florence into her narrative, the historical part is unconvincing; the episode of Savonarola is seen to be an excrescence; and what remains erect now is a wholly imaginary trinity — the noble figure of Romola, the pretty womanliness of little Tessa, and the easy-going Tito, with his moral fiber slowly disintegrating under succes-

sive temptations. Tito is one of the great triumphs of modern fiction, not because he is a
Greek of the Renascence, but because he is eternal
and to be found whenever and wherever man
lacks strength to resist himself.

If we were thus to go down the list of so-called
historical novels, one by one, we might discover
that those which were most solidly rooted in our
regard and affection are to be included in the subdivision wherein history itself is only a casual
framework for a searching study of human character, and that they are cherished for the very
same qualities as are possessed by the great novels of modern life. Without going so far as to
say that the best historical novel is that which
has the least history, we may at least confess the
frank inferiority of the other subdivision in which
the author has been rash enough to employ historical scene and character to make his own
work attractive. What gives charm and value to
'Henry Esmond' is exactly what gives charm
and value to 'Vanity Fair' — Thackeray's understanding of his fellow-man, his sympathetic insight into human nature, his happy faculty for
dramatically revealing character by situation.
Perhaps the eighteenth-century atmosphere, with
which Thackeray was able to surround Esmond
only by infinite skill, is not breathed comfortably
by the most of those who enjoy the book for its

23

manly qualities. One feels that the author has won
his wager—but at what a cost, and at what a risk!

Some logical readers of this essay may be
moved to put two and two together, and to
accuse the present writer of a desire to disparage
the historical novel, because he has tried to
show, first, that the novelists cannot reproduce
in their pages the men and women of another
epoch as these really thought and felt, and, second, that the novelists who have attempted historical fiction have best succeeded when they
brought the fiction to the center of the stage and
left the history in the background. But to draw
this conclusion would be unjust, since the writer
really agrees with the views of Sainte-Beuve as
expressed in a letter to Champfleury: "The novel
is a vast field of experiment, open to all the forms
of genius. It is the future epic, the only one,
probably, that modern manners will hereafter
justify. Let us not bind it too tightly; let us
not lay down its theory too rigidly; let us not
organize it."

To point out that a historical novel is great—
when it is great—because of its possession of
the identical qualities that give validity to a
study of modern life, is not to suggest that only
the contemporary novel is legitimate. To dwell
on the deficiencies of the historical novel is not
to propose that only realistic fiction be tolerated

hereafter. But perhaps a due consideration of these inherent defects of the historical novel may lead the disinterested reader to confess its essential inferiority to the more authentic fiction, in which the story-teller reports on humanity as he actually sees it. And if Romance is preferred to Realism, Romance is purest when purged of all affectation.

Genuine Romance is always as delightful as shoddy Romanticism is always detestable. Fantasy is ever beautiful, when it presents itself frankly as fantasy. 'Undine' does not pretend to accuracy; and the 'Arabian Nights' never vaunted itself as founded on the facts of Haroun-al-Rashid's career. Stevenson's romances, artistically truthful, though they contradict the vulgar facts of every-day existence,—'Markheim,' for example, and the 'Strange Case of Dr. Jekyll and Mr. Hyde,'—bid fair to outlive his Romanticist admixtures of Scott and Dumas; and the 'New Arabian Nights,' with its matter-of-fact impossibility, will outweigh the 'Master of Ballantrae' a dozen times over. But pure Romance and frank fantasy are strangely rare; there are very few Hoffmanns and Fouqués, Poes and Stevensons, in a century — and only one Hawthorne.

Not long ago an enterprising American journalist wrote to some twoscore of the story-tellers of Great Britain and of the United States to inquire

what, in their opinion, the object of the novel **was.** Half a dozen of the replies declared that it was "to realize life"; and the rest — an immense majority — were satisfied to say that it was "to amuse." Here we see the practitioners of the art divided in defining its purpose; and a like diversity of opinion can be detected among the vast army of novel-readers. Some think that fiction ought to be literature, and that "literature is a criticism of life." Some hold that fiction is mere story-telling — the stringing together of adventure, the heaping up of excitement, with the wish of forgetting life as it is, of getting outside of the sorry narrowness of sordid and commonplace existence into a fairy-land of dreams where Cinderella always marries Prince Charming and where the haughty sisters always meet with their just punishment. It is to readers of this second class that the ordinary historical novel appeals with peculiar force; for it provides the drug they desire, while they can salve their conscience during this dissipation with the belief that they are, at the same time, improving their minds. The historical novel is aureoled with a pseudo-sanctity, in that it purports to be more instructive than a mere story: it claims — or at least the claim is made in its behalf — that it is teaching history. There are those who think that it thus adds hypocrisy to its other faults.

Bagehot — and there is no acuter critic of men and books, and none with less literary bias — Bagehot suggested that the immense popularity of 'Ivanhoe' was due to the fact that "it describes the Middle Ages as we should wish them to be." This falsification characteristic of the historical novel in general is one of its chief charms in the eyes of those who like to be ravished out of themselves into an illusion of a world better than the one they, unfortunately, have to live in. "All sensible people know that the Middle Ages must have been very uncomfortable," continues Bagehot. "No one knew the abstract facts on which this conclusion rests better than Scott; but his delineation gives no general idea of the result: a thoughtless reader rises with the impression that the Middle Ages had the same elements of happiness which we have at present, and that they had fighting besides." Scott knew better, of course; but though "when aroused, he could take a distinct view of the opposing facts, he liked his own mind to rest for the most part in the same pleasing illusion." Perhaps Bagehot might have agreed with some later critics who have held that many of Scott's novels are immoral because of this falsification of historic truth — a charge which receives no support from the 'Bride of Lammermoor,' for example, nor from the 'Heart of Midlothian,' and half a dozen other of his stories, in which Scott's strong sense of reality and his fine feeling for Romance are displayed in perfect harmony.

(1897)

II

ROMANCE AGAINST
ROMANTICISM

ROMANCE AGAINST ROMANTICISM

AN obvious advantage which science possesses over art is that its vocabulary is precise and exact. When a man of science has occasion to use terms like Horse-power, Foot-ton, Peroxid, Volt, not only does he himself know absolutely what he himself means, but he can be confident that those whom he addresses must also know absolutely what he means. These scientific terms may be awkward or ugly,—as indeed many of them are,—but nevertheless they are accepted as having an unchanging content. They never suggest more or less at one time than at another. They pass current everywhere at their face-value; the rate of exchange never varies. But the terms which any critic of art must use lack this useful rigidity; they are ever flexible, not to say fluid. They are all things to all men. They are chameleons, changing color while we gaze at them. They are modified by the personality of the user first of all, and then by that of every several individual among those he is addressing. The epithet which to one savors of eulogy to another reeks with opprobrium. The word which is a term of reproach in the mouth of a speaker belonging to one school is a badge of honor at the hands of an adherent of another theory. When, for example, have any two theoreticians of esthetics ever agreed on a definition of beauty? When have any two critics of literature ever accepted the same definition of poetry? We may each of us think that he understands the difference between Classic and Romantic, between Romantic and Realistic, between Realistic and Idealistic, and between Realistic and Naturalistic; but any of us would be sadly rash if he should expect that the half or the quarter of those he was trying to reach understood this antithesis or that exactly as he did. In all artistic discussion the meaning each of the disputants attaches to the special words he is using is the final expression of his personal equation.

Although there is really no hope that any scientific precision will ever be attained in the terminology of esthetics or that men of letters will ever agree on the meaning they will attach to important words, discussion may help to bring about clearer knowledge. Especially may it lead to a sharper differentiation between words often loosely regarded as synonymous. Few

lovers of poetry, who desire not merely to enjoy
but seek also to understand and appreciate,
would deny the abiding value of the distinction
between fancy and the imagination — a distinction first insisted upon by the Lake Poets a scant
century ago.

Who was it who said that every man was
born either a Platonist or an Aristotelian, whether
he knew it or not? So, in another sense, must
every man be born either a Greek or a Goth.
His native temperament either forces him to
accept the Latin tradition of restraint and mod-
eration, or else it urges him to follow rather the
Teutonic ideal of individuality and self-assertion.
If he is really interested in life, he cannot choose
but enlist in the one camp or the other, however
strong his desire to preserve a benevolent neu-
trality. And what he is in matters of public pol-
icy he is likely to be in his private tastes also.
Either he delights in the Classic or else he prefers
the Romantic: for him to be an Eclectic is a stark
impossibility; and it is only the few who care
nothing for the cause of the quarrel who can
raise the cry, "A plague on both your houses!"

But among those who delight in the Classic
there is no unanimity in declaring just what the
Classic is: and there is even greater disagreement among those who prefer the Romantic as
to the full meaning of the word. The first chap-

ter of Professor Beers's illuminative 'History of English Romanticism' is taken up with an attempt to collect and to classify the manifold definitions of the spirit which animated the Romantic movement in Germany and France and England; and in all the various histories of literature in all the various modern languages it would be difficult to discover a chapter more interesting or more instructive; and a careful perusal of it may be recommended to every historian of literary development who persists dogmatically in using the terms of esthetic criticism as though they had a scientific precision.

Professor Beers quotes Heine's assertion that "all the poetry of the Middle Ages has a certain definite character, through which it differs from the poetry of the Greeks and Romans," and that "in reference to this difference, the former is called Romantic, the latter Classic," although these names "are misleading and have caused the most vexatious confusion." One reason why these terms are misleading is that in our ordinary use of the two words we are accustomed to find in Classic a certain worthiness, as of abiding merit, whereas in Romantic we feel a certain unworthiness, as conveying at least a flavor of extravagance or freakishness. Thus we say that Angelica Kauffmann's marriage was "very romantic," and that Lincoln's Gettysburg Address is "truly a classic." And Pater, taking a hint perhaps from this ordinary use of words, came to the conclusion that the Classic has "order in beauty," and the Romantic "strangeness added to beauty."

So Professor Beers keeps on assembling and comparing the criterions proposed successively for determining the essential quality of the Romantic. "First it was mystery, then aspiration; now it is the appeal to the emotions by the method of suggestion. And yet there is, perhaps, no inconsistency on the critic's part in this continual shifting of his ground. He is apparently presenting different facets of the same truth; he means one thing by his mystery, aspiration, indefiniteness, incompleteness, emotional suggestiveness; that quality or effect which we all feel to be present in Romantic and absent from Classical work."

Perhaps it is rash for any one to venture a further effort to distinguish more precisely things which we all recognize as dissimilar, not to say antithetic. But it may not be adding to the confusion to assert that those of us who seek in a work of art specially the normal and the typical presented with rigorous severity of form are on the side of the Classics, no matter what we may choose to call ourselves; and that, on the other hand, those of us who relish rather the abnormal and the unusual revealed with incomplete suggestiveness are to be counted with the Romantics, whatever we ourselves may declare. On the one side are those who enjoy simplicity and worship beauty, and on the other are those who prefer complexity, and who get their pleasure from the picturesque. As it happens, the noblest examples of simple beauty are Greek, and the finest illustrations of complex picturesqueness are medieval. But whether it is the Parthenon or Notre Dame, whether it is the work of the Athenians or of the Parisians, a masterpiece of the Classic or a masterpiece of the Romantic is always the direct and honest expression of the men who wrought it.

But the high merit of these masterpieces has attracted imitators, lacking in sincerity and not seeking to express themselves directly or honestly. Of course it is right and proper in all the arts that the young should model themselves at first on their elders and betters, learning all these have to teach, and beginning where these left off; but this fertile acceptance is as different as may be from sterile copying of formulas. One is a free-hand drawing and the other is a mere mechanical tracing.

Classic denotes imperishable beauty, while Classicism (to me at least) connotes a frigid imitation. Classic is free, while Classicism is bound.

Shakspere is the great English classic; but Classicism in English literature is embodied in Pope. So Romance is genuine, while Romanticism is pinchbeck. True Romance, whether ancient or medieval or modern, is as sincere and as direct and as honest as the Classic itself. And it needs to be distinguished sharply from Romanticism, which is often insincere, generally indirect, and sometimes artistically dishonest. Just as we need to set off sham Classicism from the noble Classic, so we ought to dwell on the essential difference between Romance and its bastard brother Romanticism—between the genuine Romantic and the imitative Romanticist.

The Romantic calls up the idea of something primary, spontaneous, and perhaps medieval, while the Romanticist suggests something secondary, conscious, and of recent fabrication. Romance, like many another thing of beauty, is very rare; but Romanticism is common enough nowadays. The truly Romantic is difficult to achieve; but the artificial Romanticist is so easy as to be scarce worth the attempting. The Romantic is ever young, ever fresh, ever delightful; but the Romanticist is stale and second-hand and unendurable. Romance is never in danger of growing old, for it deals with the spirit of man without regard to times and seasons; but Romanticism gets out of date with every twist of the kaleidoscope of literary fashion. The Romantic is eternally and essentially true, but the Romanticist is inevitably false. Romance is sterling, but Romanticism is shoddy.

It may be admitted that this distinction between the Romantic and the Romanticist is not self-evident, and that it is not always easily apprehended. Perhaps his failure to bring it out clearly and to emphasize it is one reason why Mr. Howells's attitude toward Romance has been misunderstood and that he has been accused of intolerance and even of attack, when it is only barren Romanticism he detests and despises, and when he has more than once gladly recorded his delight in true Romance. Difficult it is always to expose a sham, without seeming to be disrespectful toward that which it degrades by its mimicry. So the unsparing laying bare of hypocrisy in Molière's 'Tartuffe' was held by many good people to be little better than an assault on the church itself.

It was Mill who said that "the truth of poetry is to paint the human soul truly," and that "the truth of fiction is to give a true picture of life." Romance, however, detached from the accidental and encumbering facts of existence, is always in accord with the essential truth of life. Romance never contradicts reality, whereas Romanticism is in constant disaccord not merely with fact but

even more with truth itself. The elder Hawthorne was a writer of Romance and the elder
Dumas was a compounder of Romanticism; and
it was the author of the 'House of the Seven
Gables' who asserted that Romance, "while as a
work of art it must rigidly subject itself to laws,
and while it sins unpardonably so far as it may
swerve aside from the truth of the human heart,
has fairly a right to present that truth under circumstances to a great extent of the writer's own
choosing or creation."

Here Hawthorne asks no release from the eternal verities, but insists on permission to deal with
brave translunary things, and to lay the scene of
his story in the Forest of Arden or in the Bohemia which is a desert country by the sea, illu-
mined by a light that never was and echoing
with battles long ago. But how far are these
enchanted realms from the topsy-turvy territory
where the throng of disciples of Dumas invite us
to follow — a strange place indeed, where happy
accidents and marvelous coincidences and special providences happen many times a day. It
is in fact an undiscovered country from whose
bourn no traveler returns — except to tell trav-
elers' tales. It is a kingdom where dwell blame-
less heroes of a perfect courage who strive with
villains of an abhorrent turpitude and who adore
scornful ladies of an ethereal beauty. In a region

inhabited by these unnatural monsters, what chances of acceptance have the eternal verities ?— what possibility is there for a true picture of life or for a true painting of the human soul ?

For these shabby puppets of the worn-out Romanticist true Romance cares nothing, needing no more than a man and a maid and a spring morning. Romance is in the heart of man, and not in the circus-trappings of pseudo-history. Romance is, in the nature of things, young and eternal: it is not a machine-made output of a fiction-factory. Romance is not necessarily one

> who discerns
> No character or glory in his times,
> And trundles back his soul five hundred years,
> Past moat and drawbridge, into a castle-court.

Romance is not a thing that lived yesterday and is dead to-day — although it blossoms in the twilight atmosphere of Once upon a Time. Romance has no more to do with the tilting at Ashby-de-la-Zouch than it has to do with a corner on the Stock Exchange: it has to do with men, medieval or modern, no matter — with men as they go forth to do their duty, to be tempted and lured, to conquer the lust of the flesh, to fall into sin and to pay the penalty, to make the brave fight, be the end of the struggle what it may. Romance is where men are, with the passions and strivings of men; and it takes no account of costume and of furniture and of the accidental accompaniments of human existence.

Romance lived with the Cave-men and the Lake-folk; with the Norseman and the Crusader; with the Cavalier and the Puritan; with the Minute-men of Lexington and with the Young Guard at Waterloo; with every man who is stout of soul and who has an eye for a pretty girl; with every woman who is, or hopes to be, a wife and a mother. "Where heart-blood beat or hearth-smoke curled," there Romance wove his spell.

> "Romance!" the season tickets mourn.
> "He never ran to catch his train,
> But passed with coach and guard and horn—
> And left the local—late again!
> Confound Romance!" And all unseen
> Romance brought up the nine-fifteen.
>
> His hand was on the lever laid,
> His oil-can soothed the worrying cranks,
> His whistle waked the snow-bound grade,
> His fog-horn cut the reeking Banks:
> By dock and deep and mine and mill
> The Boy-god, reckless, labored still!

And after this quotation in verse from Mr. Kipling, let me make another in prose from Mr. Stevenson: "True romantic art again makes a Romance of all things. It reaches into the highest abstraction of the ideal; it does not refuse the most pedestrian Realism. 'Robinson Crusoe' is as realistic as it is romantic: both qualities are pushed to an extreme, and neither suffers. Nor does Romance depend upon the material importance of the incidents. To deal with strong and deadly elements, banditti, pirates, war, and murder, is to conjure with great names, and, in the event of failure, double the disgrace. The arrival of Haydn and Consuelo at the Canon's villa is a very trifling incident: yet we may read a dozen boisterous stories from beginning to end, and not receive so fresh and stirring an impression of adventure."

This is Romance as Stevenson saw it; and Romanticism is not like unto this. Romanticism is feebly fond of the "strong and deadly elements, banditti, pirates, war, and murder"—the stage-properties and supernumeraries of the pseudo-historic. The 'Bride of Lammermoor' is Romance indeed and of a lofty type: but is not 'Ivanhoe' contaminated with mere Romanticism? Now and again Dickens struck the true note, but only infrequently; and the 'Tale of Two Cities,' with the immoral self-sacrifice at the core of it, is Romanticism in its most tortuous type. Hawthorne is less likely to go astray than most: he is sometimes somewhat over-insistent on his fantasy, but he never slips headlong into the slough of Romanticism. His footing is more secure in the 'Blithedale Romance' than in the 'Marble Faun.' He complained that there was as yet here in America no "Faery Land, so like the real world that in suitable remoteness one cannot well tell the difference, but with an atmosphere of strange enchantment, beheld through which the inhabitants have a propriety of their own"— and yet we all see a solid certainty in his Brook Farm, while few can help feeling a faint unreality in his Rome.

The truly Romantic is not morbid; rather is it sane and sunny, even if the clouds gather in time and the light is quenched at last. But the Romanticist, where it is not merely foolish, is often sickly, as Goethe said, contrasting Romanticism with the Classic. To a student of German literature, Romanticism suggests 1802 and the blue flower of Novalis. To a student of French literature, Romanticism evokes 1830 and the red waistcoat of Gautier. And it was Goethe again who dismissed 'Hernani' as absurd. True Romance there is in both languages, 'Undine' in the one and the 'Princess of Cleves' in the other, for example: but in neither language is the Romanticist ever really healthy. In German there is an obvious tendency to degenerate into mere gush: and in French there is an equally obvious tendency toward illegality. Hugo and Dumas were prone to exalt the outlaw; and it was

Thiers who declared that the Communists of 1871 were only the Romanticists of 1830.

This note of revolt is to be heard more particularly in the Romanticism of France, although it is at times audible also in England; it is resonant enough in Byron. But the special peculiarity of the heroes of English Romanticism is their lack of common sense. They are feeble folk, most of them, the pale spirits evoked by Keats and Shelley, mooning foolishly through a useless existence. "Uncanny creatures," they have been called, "spectral, prone to posing, psychologically shallow." But the heroes of Romance, of true Romance, are not of this sort; they are brave boys, all of them, hearty and honest and sturdy. Are not Romeo and Orlando heroes of Romance? and are they spectral or uncanny? Orlando, it is true, roamed the forest, hanging verses on the melancholy boughs; but he was a fine fellow for all that—a good trencherman of a certainty, and could try a fall on occasion. And Romeo, consumed by passion as he was, is no dreamy milksop, but a full-blooded man, prompt to overleap a garden wall and ready to

> seal with a righteous kiss
> A dateless bargain to engrossing death.

The Romanticist is not seldom as sickly as it is shallow, but the truly Romantic is always

wholesome. Indeed, it may even be bracing —
who ever felt any relaxing of fiber after reading
the 'Scarlet Letter'? It charms and it gives an
exquisite pleasure, but it does not enervate or
disintegrate like Romanticist fictions. It may be
tonic; it is never anodyne. Mr. Howells was
not thinking of true Romance, but of the false
Romanticism, when he expressed his contempt
for the stories that are intended to take the
reader's mind off himself and to "make one forget life and all its cares and duties," and that
"are not in the least like the novels which make
you think of these, and shame you into at least
wishing to be a helpfuller and wholesomer creature than you are." And then Mr. Howells with
ill-restrained scorn discusses the Romanticist
fictions with no sordid details of verity, "no
wretched being humbly and weakly struggling
to do right and to be true, suffering for his follies
and his sins, tasting joy only through the mortifi-
cation of self and in the help of others; nothing
of all this: but a great, whirling splendor of peril
and achievement, a wild scene of heroic adventure, and of emotional ground and lofty tumbling,
with a stage picture at the fall of the curtain, and
all the good characters in a row, their left hands
pressed upon their hearts, and kissing their right
hands to the audience."

To try to point out the difference between the

truly Romantic and its illegitimate younger brother, the artificial Romanticist, is not to indulge in a vain dispute about terms; it is to accomplish the needful task of bringing out the essential distinction between two things often carelessly confused. Even though Romanticism is not the best possible word to identify the ape of genuine Romance, it remains the best word available for the purpose. As we have no warrant to make new words at will, we must needs differentiate an old word by a new use. Whatever the word that shall finally win acceptance as describing the thing here called Romanticism, there can be no doubt that the thing itself needs to be set apart from Romance. Already do we distinguish between fancy and imagination, between wit and humor—although here both of the objects thus set off one from another are worthy. How much more needful, then, is it for us to set off Romanticism from Romance just so soon as we see clearly that only Romance is really worthy and that Romanticism is obviously unworthy of association with it.

(1900)

III

NEW TRIALS FOR OLD FAVORITES

NEW TRIALS FOR OLD FAVORITES

IN the book of travels which he has called 'Following the Equator,' Mark Twain casually speaks of the 'Vicar of Wakefield' as "that strange menagerie of complacent hypocrites and idiots, of theatrical Cheap-John heroes and heroines who are always showing off, of bad people who are not interesting, and of good people who are fatiguing." And the iconoclastic humorist, not satisfied with this sweeping censure, goes further, and calls Goldsmith's masterpiece "a singular book," with "not a sincere line in it; a book which is one long waste-pipe discharge of goody-goody puerilities and dreary moralities; a book which is full of pathos which revolts, and of humor which grieves the heart."

This is strong language; and with all due respect for the clearness of vision which Mark Twain has often revealed in dealing with literature, as in dealing with life itself, and with a full recognition of the implacable common sense which is always his chief characteristic, I cannot but think that he has here overstated his case against Goldsmith, as he once overstated his case against Cooper. The sentence of annihilation which he passes upon the 'Vicar of Wakefield' is as severe as that which he passed upon the Leatherstocking Tales; and they both of them seem to suggest rather the glad exaggeration of the wanton humorist than the severe restraint of the cautious critic.

And yet it may be noted that Mr. Austin Dobson, the latest biographer of Goldsmith, had frankly admitted in advance not a few of the charges which Mark Twain has harshly urged. Mr. Dobson remarked upon the "structural inconsistencies" of the story and upon "its naïve neglect of probability"; and he asked: "Where, in the world about us, do events succeed each other in such convenient sequence? Where do persons answer to their names with such opportune precision?" And he confessed also that "we may gape a little over some of its old-fashioned maxims. . . . We may even think Squire Thornhill a little too much of the stage-libertine; we may have our doubts touching that ubiquitous philanthropist, his uncle."

Where the British critic would join issue with the American humorist is in traversing the charge that there is "not a sincere line in it," since sincerity is the very quality not to be denied to the

genial Irishman. And when Mark Twain insists
that the good characters in the little tale are all
fatiguing, it is well to recall that Mr, Dobson finds
the family of Wakefield to be like Dryden's milk-
white hind, "immortal and unchanged," and that
he holds them to be "such friendly, such accustomed figures, they are so fixed and settled in our
intimacy, that we have forgotten to remember
how good they are—how clearly and roundly
realized, how winningly and artlessly presented."

Mr. Dobson is not one of the biographers who
get their saint only because they refuse to allow
free speech and fair play to the devil's advocate;
and he appreciates fully Voltaire's saying, that
criticism of detail is never fatal. Voltaire elsewhere asserted that the critic does not know his
trade who cannot discover the causes of a book's
success; and Mr. Dobson has pointed out the real
reasons why the ' Vicar of Wakefield ' has pleased
long and pleased many, in spite of its obvious
shortcomings. Goldsmith presented the Primrose family so simply and so sympathetically that
the world was delighted to take them to its heart,
notwithstanding the clumsiness of the plot and
the staginess of many of the personages. We
can now detect in Dr. Primrose a certain eighteenth-century attitude toward the established
order in church and in state which is not pleasing in our nineteenth-century eyes, and which is

probably the cause of Mark Twain's contemptuous accusation of " complacent hypocrisy "; but,
in spite of this, the record of the Vicar's little
vanities and little weaknesses is not fatiguing,
and the Vicar himself lingers in our memory as a
Christian gentleman.

Mark Twain is a good workman; but he is not
unwilling to carry one of his chips on his shoul-
der. He has a hatred of humbug almost as hearty
as Molière's, and a scorn of hypocrisy almost as
hot; and it may be that he was moved to this
violent outbreak in protest against the unthinking
lip-reverence with which books like the ' Vicar of
Wakefield ' are treated generally. Any one who
truly loves literature, and who takes a real interest
in its history, can hardly fail to be annoyed by the
superstitious veneration paid to the minor masterpieces of the past. They are mentioned with
bated breath, as though they were flawless gems,
to hint a spot on which were akin to sacrilege.
It is the very negation of criticism to act on the
theory that even the great poets were impeccable, that Homer never nodded and that Shakspere
never slept; and a willingness to close the eyes
resolutely to all the weak points in their works
may lead in time to an inability to see where
their real strength lies. And if it is safest for
the honest critic not to blind himself to the fact
that in ' Hamlet,' in the fifth act especially, there

are still obvious traces of the earlier and inferior
tragedy-of-blood upon which it was founded, and
that in ' Don Quixote ' the pretense of a translated
manuscript is tedious and ill sustained, so it is
doubly important that the honest critic should
keep his eyes open wide when he comes to deal
with the lesser classics, with books like the ' Vicar
of Wakefield' and 'Gil Blas' and 'Paul and Virginia'
—books each of which has a place of its own in the
complex development of the modern novel, but
for which it is absurd to claim verbal inspiration.

Goldsmith's domestic idyl suggested Goethe's
' Hermann and Dorothea,' and, indirectly, Longfellow's ' Evangeline.' Le Sage's picaresque
romance inspired Smollett's robustious ' Roderick Random '; it influenced Dickens in the ' Pickwick Papers ' and in ' Nicholas Nickleby '; and it
even provided an unconscious model for Mark
Twain's ' Tom Sawyer ' and ' Huckleberry Finn.'
Saint-Pierre's exotic love-story revealed to later
novelists the possibility of making the forces of
nature—the flowers of the field and the winds of
heaven—play a part in the tragedy of life. The
' Vicar of Wakefield ' and ' Gil Blas ' and ' Paul
and Virginia ' are all of them important in the
history of fiction, for one reason or another; but
they are none of them so mighty in their scope
that we need be afraid to weigh their merits exactly and to measure their faults with precision.

We are justified in insisting on a careful examination, not only of their credentials from the past, but of the works themselves. They come to us with the indorsement of preceding generations; but we gave no preceding generation a power of attorney to decide what we should like in literature, or to declare what we must admire. Every generation exercises the right of private judgment for itself. Every generation is a Court of Appeals, which never hesitates to overrule and reverse the judgments of its predecessors. When a book has been praised since a time whereof the memory of man runneth not to the contrary, the probability is large that the commendation is deserved. But there is always a possibility that its reputation has been preserved merely because the book has become unreadable and has thus tempted nobody to explode its inherited fame.

We have always a right to reopen the case whenever fresh evidence is discovered. In the Court of Criticism there is no doctrine of *stare decisis*: precedent cannot estop the action of posterity. Nothing is more unwholesome for a living literature than a willingness to accept a tradition without question, blindfold and obedient. Nothing is worse for the welfare of a living literature than an acceptance of that maxim of Pudd'n'head Wilson's, in which he asserts that a classic is a book everybody praises and nobody reads, unless it is an acting upon the maxim of Samuel Rogers, who said that whenever a new book came out he read an old one. We need the new and the old; but we need the old for what it is to us now, and not for what it was to readers of the last century.

When Mr. Howells aroused the rage of the British lion by his innocent suggestion that the art of fiction is a finer art nowadays than it had been in Thackeray's time, he was, in fact, guilty of an obvious commonplace. Guy de Maupassant may or may not be a better shot than Honoré de Balzac, but there is no doubt as to the superiority of the younger writer's rifle. So Thackeray himself had a better gun than Scott; and Scott could have had a better gun than Fielding, although for some reason he apparently preferred the old-fashioned bow of yew with its cloth-yard arrow. No wonder is it, therefore, that some readers of to-day, accustomed to the feats of long-range marksmanship made possible by the latest weapons of precision, are often impatient at the results of the target-practice of our ancestors.

Scott declared that few have read 'Gil Blas' "without remembering, as one of the most delightful occupations of their life, the time which they first employed in its perusal"; and he goes further, and suggests that "if there is anything like truth in Gray's opinion, that to lie upon a couch and read new novels was no bad idea of Paradise, how would that beatitude be enhanced could human genius afford us another 'Gil Blas'!" Thackeray asserted that "the novel of 'Humphrey Clinker' is, I do think, the most laughable story that has been written since the goodly art of novel-writing began." Coleridge maintained that the three finest plots in the whole history of literature were to be found in the 'Œdipus' of Sophocles, the 'Alchemist' of Ben Jonson, and the 'Tom Jones' of Fielding.

Scott and Thackeray and Coleridge are critics whose equipment and insight and disinterestedness every lover of literature must respect. But Coleridge died before the modern novel had reached its full development, and if he overpraised the plot of 'Tom Jones,' it was perhaps because he could not foresee the 'Scarlet Letter' or 'Smoke.' No doubt Thackeray relished the eighteenth century exceedingly; but when he singled out 'Humphrey Clinker' as a masterpiece of laughter-making, he could have had no premonition of 'Tom Sawyer' and of 'Tartarin on the Alps.' And in like manner Scott's eulogy of 'Gil Blas' falls on deaf ears now that it is addressed to those who have feasted their eyes on the far more varied panorama provided in the Waverley Novels.

Much of our veneration for the classics is a sham, the result, in part, of our sheep-like unwillingness to think for ourselves. Follow-my-leader is the game most of us play when we are called upon to declare our preferences. We put 'Tom Jones,' for example, into our lists of the Hundred Best Books—lists, for the most part, as fatuous as they are absurd; but if we were honest with ourselves, as I suppose we should be if the choice was actual, very few of us would pack 'Tom Jones' in the chest we express to the mythical desolate island. There is no doubt that 'Tom Jones' is a great novel, one of the greatest in our language, and perhaps one of the greatest in the modern literature of any country. It has form and substance; it is admirably planned and beautifully written; it abounds in humor and in irony and in knowledge of human nature; it is peopled by a company of living men and women; it reveals to us a most manly character, the character of Henry Fielding himself—sturdy, honest, and sincere, clear-eyed and plain-spoken. The book is eternal in its verity, and therefore in its interest; but it has the remote morality of the eighteenth century, and the hardness of tone of that unlovely era; it belongs to an earlier stage in the development of fiction; it demands for its full enjoyment a certain measure of culture in its readers; and therefore it is becoming year by year

more and more a novel for the few, and less and
less a novel for the many.

As with 'Tom Jones' so with 'Don Quixote'
—a greater book, making a wider appeal, and not
bounded by the horizon of a single century. The
carelessness with which Cervantes put his story
together, the fortuitous adventures and the in-
congruous meetings—these things are of little
consequence; for, as George Sand aptly put it,
"the best books are not those with the fewest
faults, but those with the greatest merits." The
merits of 'Don Quixote' are great beyond dispute;
but are they such as can be appreciated by that
impossible entity, the Average Reader? Spain's
chivalry has been laughed away so thoroughly
that nowadays a man must needs have studied in
the schools to understand the circumstances of
Cervantes's satire. The genuine appreciation of
'Don Quixote'—and of 'Tom Jones' also—calls
for a preparation that few readers of fiction possess, and for an effort which few of them are inclined to make.

If this is true, is it not best to admit it frankly
—to say honestly that the 'Vicar of Wakefield'
is a tissue of improbabilities, that Gil Blas, in the
course of his rambles, happens upon much that
is no longer entertaining, and that 'Humphrey
Clinker' is not the most amusing volume now
available? The penalty for not speaking the truth

boldly is pretty serious. It consists in the very real danger that he who is enticed by traditional eulogy to attempt these books and others like them, and who recoils with disappointment, as many a time he must, will thereafter distrust his judgment, and will be inclined to suppose that literature is something hard, something dull, something repellent, something beyond his reach.

When Mr. Reed defined a statesman as "a successful politician who is dead," he voiced a sentiment very like that which rules many of our literary guides. In their minds, nothing is literature that was not written either in a dead language or by a dead man, and everything is literature which was written by a dead man in a dead language. They praise the old books which they either read with an effort or do not read at all; and it rarely occurs to them to analyze the source of their pleasure in the new books which they read with joy. 'Huckleberry Finn,' for example, has been devoured with delight by hundreds of thousands of Americans; but the rare references to it in print are most of them doubtful and patronizing.

Now 'Huckleberry Finn' contains the picture of a civilization nowhere else adequately recorded in literature: it abounds in adventure and in character, in fun and in philosophy. It appears to me to be a work of extraordinary merit, and a better book of the same kind than 'Gil Blas,' richer in humor, and informed by a riper humanity. But Mark Twain's story is a book of to-day, and it is American; it is not a book of yesterday and foreign; it can be enjoyed by anybody, even by a boy, and it seems to make no demand on the understanding. There is no tradition of laudation encompassing it about, and it is not sanctified by two centuries of eulogy. It is easy for us to read, since the matter is familiar and the manner also; but it is difficult for us to praise, since the critics who preceded us have not set us the example.

Probably it was at a new opera that Rufus Choate besought his daughter to interpret to him the libretto, lest he dilate with the wrong emotion. At all the old operas every man of us knows with what emotion it is that he ought to dilate, since we are prone to accept the tradition, if only to save us the trouble of thinking for ourselves. To arouse us from our laziness and our lethargy there is nothing like a vehement assault on the inherited opinion—even if the charge is too sweeping, like Mark Twain's annihilation of Goldsmith's little masterpiece.

If a study of the history of literature reveals anything clearly, it is that a reversal of the judgments of our ancestors, or at least a revision, after argument, is a condition of progress. If the old favorites cannot stand a new trial, there may be a recommendation to mercy; but there is no doubt about the verdict. For us to advance in the right path, we must look at literature, as we look at life, with our own eyes, and not through the spectacles of our grandfathers. The critics of the Renascence in every country of Europe were united in holding that the model of the drama had been set by the Greeks once for all, and that this model was in no wise to be modified or departed from; and the insistence on this theory deprived Italy of a drama of its own, and came desperately near to strangling the drama of England and that of Spain. Fortunately, the populace of London and of Madrid were not awed by the authority of criticism; they knew what they wanted; they refused to accept the kind of play that had pleased the Greeks but did not happen to please them; and they would not rest satisfied till they had Shakspere and Calderon.

In the lapse of time Calderon and Shakspere got themselves slowly accepted as classics, but after how hard a struggle in the case of Shakspere!—a struggle ending in the triumph of the dramatist only toward the end of the eighteenth century and with the revival of the romantic. No department of literary history is, I think, more instructive, and none, I am sure, tends more to teach us humility, than the record of the fluctuations in the fame of one or another of the masters of literature—such a record as Professor Lounsbury has given us in one of his luminous 'Studies of Chaucer.' Each of these masters has had his eclipses, from which he has emerged at last; and many of the minor bards have had, each in his turn, their periods of effulgence, now come to an end forever. For nearly a century Shakspere was held to be inferior to Ben Jonson; and for an even longer period Homer was held in lower esteem than the smoother Vergil.

Two or three hundred years ago the Italians used to speak of the Four Poets, meaning Dante, Petrarch, Ariosto, and Tasso; and in those days the rest of the civilized world was ready enough to admit the supremacy of this quartet. The canon of to-day also admits four poets—Homer, Dante, Shakspere, and Goethe. We who speak English may wish to add Milton as a fifth; they who speak French might claim admission for Hugo instead; while the Latins would put in a plea for the inclusion of Vergil. But how Voltaire would have scoffed at any list that included the Gothic Dante and the barbarian Shakspere! And how Voltaire's followers, the little German critics who came before Lessing, would have shrieked with horror at the omission of Pope, Boileau, and Horace! I wonder sometimes whether some of our opinions—even those upon which all the authoritative critics of our time are united—will not strike the more enlightened twenty-first century as equally jejune. And yet I need not wonder; for few things are more certain to come about than that the future will jeer at more than one judgment of the present, just as we scoff haughtily at many of the judgments of the past. Every century—even every generation—contributes material for a new chapter on the vicissitudes of artistic reputation.

For a decade or more Byron was universally accepted as the foremost poet of all Europe. Fifty years later Byron was ranked by most British critics below Shelley and Keats and Wordsworth, no one of whom has ever had any vogue outside of his own language. Now, again, as the century draws to an end, there are plentiful signs of a revolution in Byron's favor. But if Byron ever reconquers a fame like that which he possessed just before his death, it will be by virtue of his real qualities and not by favor of accompanying faults—although his earlier notoriety seemed to be due almost as much to the latter as to the former. In like manner Lamartine is regaining to-day in France a position such as he occupied once before; only he is solidly supported now, and far better able to repel assault. So, too, Victor Hugo, against whom there was a violent reaction after his death,—a reaction perhaps not yet at an end in Paris itself,—is coming slowly to be recognized, especially by foreign critics, as the finest lyric poet of France, and even as the foremost lyrist of Europe in the nineteenth century. This recognition has been made possible only by the perspective of time, which has revealed the 'Légende des Siècles' looming aloft above the immense mass of Hugo's other verse, and far above his romances and his dramas. During a man's lifetime there is a tendency to estimate him by his average work: after he is dead and gone a juster valuation is arrived at by weighing only his best.

At Scott's death there was an outburst of eulogy—as much a testimony of admiration for the final struggle of the man as it was an expression of gratitude for the pleasure given by the author. Soon the thermometer fell, and there were signs of a frost. Then Lockhart published the biography; and Carlyle was ready with a review, the underlying tone of which was the same contemptuous envy he showed toward almost every one of his successful contemporaries. Scott's merits were real enough to withstand, on the one side, Carlyle's disparagement, and, on the other, the discredit derived from a host of clumsy imitators. Yet he seems a sadly belated critic who now praises Scott for his tournaments, or for his pinchbeck chivalry, or for any other of the medieval gauds which glittered so bravely in the eyes of those who read 'Ivanhoe' when it first came out. Scott's title to survival is seen at last to be founded, like the title of Fielding and of Le Sage and of Cervantes, on his vigorous and veracious portrayal of human character, on his truthful reproduction of the shrewd and sturdy men and women whom he knew so well and loved so dearly.

In the same way has the fame of George Eliot and of Dickens wavered for a long while, establishing itself more firmly as time winnows their writings, leaving it to rest on only the best works of each and not merely on the bulk of them. In George Eliot's case, 'Daniel Deronda' has already been dropped behind, and no longer impedes the full appreciation of 'Silas Marner'—perhaps the only one of her books which is direct and shapely. Dickens had even less sense of form than George Eliot; and yet he strove for constructive effects again and again, only to fail lamentably. This is one reason why those of his books are best liked now in which there is little or no pretense of a plot, in which, in fact, there is only a central figure serving as an excuse for the linking together of amusing characters and lively scenes. In 'Nicholas Nickleby' there is hardly any more formal framework than there is in 'Gil Blas' itself; and in 'Gil Blas' the correlation of the incidents is frankly fortuitous. In fact, 'Nicholas Nickleby' is one of the best specimens of the picaresque in our language. For many of us the 'Pickwick Papers' is the most readable of Dickens's works, because it contains the least plot and the least pathos, and because it was written with the least effort and the least striving for effect.

Dickens affords us an admirable example of the changing point of view of successive generations. In his own day the blank-verse death-beds of Little Nell and Paul Dombey were successful in drawing tears even from unsympathetic souls like Jeffrey. In our time these scenes annoy us; they are felt to be offensive; and they are apologized for even by the thick-and-thin defenders of Dickens. So, too, the "effects" which Dickens worked up conscientiously and with an immensity of pains strike us to-day as tawdry, not to say theatrical, and we feel the essential falseness of the devices which Dickens took obvious pride in.

What makes Mr. George Gissing's recent study of Dickens's method significant is the strange frankness with which the friendly critic admits the justice of the accusations brought against the earlier novelist's art, and the ingenuity with which he shows us that, in spite of all, Dickens's power is indisputable and his genius undeniable. All the characteristics of Dickens's writing which Mr. Howells has expressed his distaste for, Mr. Gissing allows to be execrable; he shows how Dickens yielded without a struggle to the popular liking for happy endings, and how he never hesitated at the most illogical transmogrification of character in order to bring this about; and then he seeks to establish Dickens's fame solidly for the future on the novelist's veracity in dealing with types of character in the lower middle class of London, denying that Mrs. Gamp is in any way exaggerated, calling her almost photographic, and declaring that the reproduction of Mrs. Varden's talk is phonographic in its accuracy. Mr. Gissing even ventures to compare Dickens with Balzac, with Victor Hugo, with Dostoyevsky, and with Daudet, finding "in Balzac a stronger intellect, but by no means a greater genius."

Mr. Gissing's essay reveals genuine insight into the principles of the novelist's art; it is modest and moderate; it is convincing. At least one reader, who would have confessed to little liking for Dickens either as a man or as an artist, laid it down with the feeling that the critic had made out his case, and that the adverse decision against Dickens must needs be revised now in the light of Mr. Gissing's argument, so cogent is this plea of confession and avoidance.

And yet a doubt arises again when we recall the pregnant saying of Joseph de Maistre, that, to judge a book, "it is enough to know by whom it is loved and by whom it is hated." Now as between Dickens and Thackeray,—to bring up again the comparison which is apparently as inevitable as it is absurd,—one may have a suspicion that the former is more admired by the weaklings and the sentimentalists, by the gently hypocritical and the morally short-sighted, while the latter pleases rather those who think for themselves and who stand firmly on their own feet and who take the world as it is. One robust British critic, whose own manners are notoriously bad, seems to me to prefer Dickens chiefly because Thackeray was a gentleman.

In comparing Dickens with Victor Hugo, Mr. Gissing sets Inspector Bucket by the side of Javert, and finds a realistic character in the British detective, and a type in the French, "an incarnation of the penal code, neither more nor less." Then he declares that 'Les Misérables' "is one of the world's great books," and admits that this "cannot be said of any one of Dickens's." This raises a most interesting question: What *are* the world's great books? Of course, the list would be drawn up very differently in different countries and in different centuries. The American list would not be quite the same as the British list, although there is identity of language and of literary tradition. Either of these English lists would diverge widely from the French. The Italian list and the Spanish would be closer to the French, and the German list would approach the English. If a score of competent critics, chosen from the chief modern languages, were empowered to select a dozen cosmopolitan classics there would be agreement only in regard to the ancients. About the moderns there would be the utmost diversity of opinion. No book of Dickens's would be put on the list, nor any book of Thackeray's, either, nor aught of Hawthorne's; while a volume of Poe's short stories might perhaps survive the discussion, and so might 'Uncle Tom's Cabin.' Perhaps 'Gil Blas' and 'Paul and Virginia' and the 'Vicar of Wakefield' would be able to make good their claims, and perhaps not. Perhaps, indeed, the only books in our language (except a play or two of Shakspere's) that are absolutely certain of insertion are the two books of our boyhood, 'Gulliver's Travels' and 'Robinson Crusoe,' both of them tales of seafaring, and both of them intimately characteristic of the stock that speaks English on the opposite shores of the Atlantic.

If the malignant Swift has any knowledge now of what is happening among the descendants of the men and women he despised and cringed before, it must feed fat his humor that the book he wrote to record his hatred of humanity survives to-day as a fairy-tale in the nursery. He meant it for gall and wormwood, and lo! it is found to be spoon-meat for babes. Books have their strange fates, like men; but surely none could be stranger than this, the very irony of circumstance.

As for 'Robinson Crusoe,' its permanence can be explained easily enough. M. de Vogüé has recently declared that the list of cosmopolitan classics must finally be restricted to two books, 'Don Quixote' and 'Robinson Crusoe.' He tells us that "other masterpieces take higher rank, from the perfection of their art or from the sublimity of their thought, but they do not address themselves to every age and to every condition; they demand for their enjoyment a mind already formed and an intellectual culture not given to every one. Cervantes and Defoe alone have solved the problem of interesting . . . the little child and the thoughtful old man, the servant-girl and the philosopher."

M. de Vogüé declares 'Don Quixote' to be the most pessimistic of books, and 'Robinson Crusoe' the most optimistic. He discovers in the first the whole history of Spain, and in the latter the true portrait of the English-speaking race. He sees in the shipwrecked solitary the type of the mythic hero of the north—stout-hearted and devout, ready with his hands, and sure of himself.

That 'Don Quixote' is a greater book than 'Robinson Crusoe' few would deny; but if the cosmopolitan classics are two, then is the Spanish masterpiece less cosmopolitan than the English, since its appeal is not so universal, and to appreciate it calls for more knowledge and more effort. A boy needs to learn what knight-errantry is before he can enter into sympathy with the hero of Cervantes and begin to make-believe with him. But what boy is there who cannot invent for himself a desert island and hostile savages? Defoe's hero is a type of all mankind; Robinson Crusoe's struggle for existence is ours also; and in his adventures we foresee our own—every man fighting for his own hand, every man with his back against the wall.

(1898)

IV

THE STUDY OF FICTION

[This address was prepared, at the request of the American Society for the Extension of University Teaching, to take its place in a course of lectures on Books and Reading, delivered in 1898–99.]

THE STUDY OF FICTION

MANY of us can remember a time—and a time not so very remote—when we would have scouted as an arrant absurdity any suggestion that literature was to be studied. Without giving thought to the question, we held it blindly as an article of faith that literature was for enjoyment only and for refreshment; and we may even have had a vague feeling that it was not quite solid enough to be matter for study—that it was, in fact, too entertaining to be taken seriously. If we chanced to recall De Quincey's suggestive distinction between the literature of knowledge and the literature of power, we might have admitted that the works belonging to the literature of knowledge—history, for example, and biography—might well be read with a desire for self-improvement; but as for the books belonging to the literature of power,—poetry and the drama, romance and the essay,—these were for recreation and for pleasure. They were no more to be studied than a sunset or a rainbow or a woman's face or anything else that is beautiful and variable.

But of late a change has come over us, and the scales have fallen from our eyes. Just as we are inquiring into the phenomena of the sunset and the rainbow, and just as we are classifying the types of female beauty, so also are we analyzing poetry, lyric and epic and tragic, and investigating the conditions of the essay and of the romance. The ballad serves as a basis for research, and so likewise does the short-story. A lilting legend still gives us joy, no doubt, but our delight is no longer unalloyed. It was Froissart who said that our sturdy English ancestors took their pleasure sadly; and if there were to-day to arrive among us an observer as acute and as sympathetic as the old chronicler, he might record that now we take our pleasure curiously, dissecting our emotions and seeking always to discover the final cause of our amusement.

Sometimes one or another of us may be led to wonder whether this later attitude is altogether satisfactory, and whether the new theory is not held a little too rigorously. There is something lacking more often than not in our effort to find a scientific foundation for our artistic appreciation, and the attempt itself may even tend to lessen our enjoyment. We have all seen editions of the masterpieces of poetry in which notes have sprung up so luxuriantly as to threaten to choke the life out of the unfortunate lyrist. Diagrams have even been devised to explain the mystery of the plays which plain people were once able to enjoy unthinkingly in the theater, a place where the task of the commentator is necessarily superfluous.

Instead of centering its attention on the fructifying kernel, much of the so-called teaching of literature to-day has to do chiefly with barren husks, with the mere dates of authors' biographies, and with the external facts of literary annals. When I see that pedants and pedagogs are cramming Milton's lesser lyrics and Shakspere's sylvan dramas down the unwilling throats of green boys and girls, I cannot but rejoice that my own school-days were past long before these newer methods were adopted. Indeed, I think myself fortunate that I had never studied literature until I was most unexpectedly called upon to teach it. I had read freely for the fun of it, finding the labor its own reward, or rather not finding it labor at all; and I had been led to look up the lives of the authors whose works interested me, and to compare one with another; but as for any formal study of literature, I hardly knew that such a thing was practised by any one.

Yet I can see now, as I look back at my own haphazard reading, that I might have been saved much time, and that my enjoyment in literature, keen as it always was, might have been sharpened if I had had some guide to show me the lines along which the drama and the novel had developed, and to suggest to me the interesting relationships of the different literary forms—a guide who could supply me with reasons for the preferences I had dumbly felt, and who might even aid me to combine these preferences into an esthetic theory of my own, or who could at least help me to discover for myself the principles underlying my preferences. Useful as such a guide would be in considering the essay, for instance, the history of which has not yet been thoroughly worked out, in no department of literature would he be more useful than in the broad field of fiction; first, because the field is so very broad and so sharply diversified, and, secondly, because the novel is still so young that there is hardly yet a tradition of criticism to aid us in the necessary classification.

I

This youth of the novel, as compared with the drama, for example, with oratory, with lyric poetry, must ever be borne in mind. There were nine muses of old in Greece, but to no one of them was committed the care of the novel, since the making of a fictitious tale in prose had not yet occurred to any of the Greek men of letters. It is easy for us to see now that it is a mere accident whether a story be told in verse or in prose, and that therefore the earliest of all romances of adventure is the 'Odyssey,' the bold and crafty Ulysses being thus the legitimate ancestor of Gil Blas the unscrupulous and of D'Artagnan the invulnerable. The art of the story-teller is ancient and honorable; but prose lags long after verse, and when our remote progenitor, the cave-dweller, anticipated the Athenian in liking to hear and to tell some new thing, it was in rime that he told it, though it might be only his own boastful autobiography. Even after the revival of letters, when Boccaccio and Chaucer rivaled one another in delicate perfection of narrative art, the Englishman chose verse often to tell the selfsame story for which the Italian had preferred prose; and it was the unrhythmic 'Vicar of Wakefield' which suggested the metrical 'Hermann and Dorothea,' just as the still earlier 'Daphnis and Chloe' in prose may have been in some measure the model of the later 'Evangeline' in verse.

The modern novel in prose may almost be called a creature of the nineteenth century. In many of its developments it is a thing of yesterday, and we do not yet quite know how to take it. Even now distinctions as essential as that between the novel and the romance and that between the novel and the short-story are imperfectly seized by many of those who discuss the art of fiction.

I was about to declare that the novel is like a younger brother who has gone forth to make his way in the world, and who has returned at last, wealthier by far than any of his elders who have lived leisurely by the family hearth. But this figure limps a little; indeed, I must confess that it is both inadequate and inaccurate. The novel is rather the heir of the ages, rich not only with the fortune of his father, but having received also legacies from various elderly relatives, old maids most of them. The novel has taken the heritage of the epic, and it is engaged in a hot dispute with the serious drama for the possession of what little property moribund tragedy may have to bequeath. It has even despoiled the essay of the character-sketch; and it has laid violent hands on the fountain of personal emotion formerly the sole property of the lyric. Not content with thus robbing poetry and the drama, the novel vaunts itself as a rival of history in recording the great deeds of the past; and it also claims the right to wield the weapons of oratory in discussing the burning questions of the present. In fact, fiction, at the end of the nineteenth century, may be likened to Napoleon at the very height of his power, when no other monarch could make sure of resting in peace upon the throne of his fathers.

This is perhaps the most striking fact in the history of the literature of the nineteenth century —this immense vogue of the novel and of the short-story. Fiction fills our monthly magazines, and it is piled high on the counters of our book-stores. Dr. Holmes once said that during the Civil War the cry of the American populace was for "bread and the newspapers." It would be an exaggeration, of course, to say that during periods of peace the cry of the fairer half of our population is for "clothes and the novel," but it is an exaggeration only; it is not a misrepresentation. Almost every year brings forth a story which has the surprising sale of a quarter of a million copies or more, while it is only once in a lifetime that a work in any other department of literature achieves so wide a circulation. Of late years there has been only one Grant's 'Personal Memoirs' to set off against a score of stories like 'Called Back,' like 'Mr. Barnes of New York,' like 'Trilby'; and the sale of the great leader's autobiography has not been the half of that of a novel written by one of the generals who served under him. In the past quarter of a century no essay in political economy (with the possible exception of 'Progress and Poverty') has really rivaled the circulation attained by 'Looking Backward'; and no theological treatise (with the possible exception of the 'Greatest Thing in the World') has had a tithe of the readers 'Robert Elsmere' had.

It was a primitive Scotchman who wanted to write the songs of a nation rather than its laws; and even in our more advanced civilization we can understand the wish, although it is perhaps easier for us Americans to be proud of the Constitution of the United States merely as literature than of 'Yankee Doodle' or of the 'Star-Spangled Banner.' But in these days, when few know how to sing and all know how to read, the story may be more potent than the lyric. When Mrs. Stowe visited the White House, Lincoln bent over her, saying, "And is this the little woman who made this big war?" A few years later the Czar told Turgenieff that the freeing of the serfs was the result of thoughts aroused in the autocrat of Russia by the reading of the novelist's story.

No doubt the effect of 'Uncle Tom's Cabin' has been equaled only by that of the 'Memoirs of a Sportsman.' But the influence of many another novel has been both wide and deep. The fiction which abides has been patterned after life, and in its turn it serves as a model to the living men and women who receive it eagerly. The shabby heroes of Balzac found many imitators in Paris in the middle of this century, just as the rakish heroes of Byron had found many imitators in London at the beginning of the century. The interaction of life on literature, and of literature again on life, is one of the most interesting of phenomena for the student of social development; and its importance is seen more clearly since the French psychologist M. Tarde has formulated what he terms the Law of Imitation, and since he has revealed how immense and how far-reaching is the force of an example placed conspicuously before men's eyes as a model. Plainer than ever before is the duty of the novelist now to set up no false ideals, to erect no impossible standards of strength or courage or virtue, to tell the truth about life as he sees it with his own eyes.

II

There are various ways in which the study of fiction may be approached. We may consider chiefly the contents of the book, its pictures of life and of manners, its disclosure of human characteristics and of national peculiarities; we may devote our attention rather to the form in which the story is cast, the way it is told, the methods of the narrator; or we may enlarge our views to cover the history of the art of fiction as it slowly broadens down from precedent to precedent, recording carefully the birth of every new species.

In the first case we should find a fertile field of inquiry if we sought to test the fulness and the accuracy with which race-characteristics are recorded in the fiction of a language—how the energy and the humor of the Anglo-Saxon stock dominate the novels of the English language; how the logic and the clearness and the wit of the French people are represented in French fiction; and how the diffuseness, the dreaminess, and the sentimentality of the Germans characterize German romance. In the second case, there would be instructive matter for comparison in setting side by side the mock-epic style of Fielding, the confidential attitude of Sterne and Thackeray, and the impassive manner of Flaubert and Maupassant. And in the third case, we should find ourselves facing many interesting questions: Who invented the detective story? Who wrote the first sea-tale? What is the earliest novel with a purpose? What is the origin of the historical novel? Who first made use of the landscape and of the weather as sustaining accompaniments of a story? How and when has the fiction of the English language been influenced by the fiction of the Italian, the Spanish, and the French? And how and when has it in turn affected the story-telling of other tongues? How far are the range and the precision of the modern novel due to these indefatigable international rivalries and to the interaction of various literatures one on the other?

Of these three ways of approach, perhaps the most satisfactory is the third, the historical; for it can easily be made to yield most of the advantages of the others. No one has yet written an adequate history of the development of the modern novel; but the material for an analysis of this most interesting evolution is abundant and accessible. Starting with the ill-told anecdotes of the 'Gesta Romanorum,' on the one hand, and on the other with the high-flown romances of chivalry, both of them frankly unreadable to-day, we can see how in Italy the former supplied the seed for the fully ripe tales of the 'Decameron,' and how in Spain the latter suggested by reaction the low-life narratives, those rambling autobiographies of thieves and beggars which are known as the picaresque romances, and which served as a model for 'Gil Blas.' We can trace the steps whereby the simplified figures of Boccaccio—mere masks of a Priest, a Husband, a Wife, for instance, labeled rather than individualized, existing solely for the sake of the adventures in which they are involved, and moving as though in a vacuum with no effort to surround themselves with an atmosphere—are succeeded by the more complicated creatures of Le Sage, with their recognizable human weaknesses.

We can note how slow was the growth of the desire for unity when we remark that master-pieces like 'Don Quixote' and 'Tom Jones' are each of them dilated and enfeebled by the injection of extraneous stories, supposed to be told by one of the characters and needlessly arresting the flow of the main narrative. We can discover how even to-day, when the beauty of unity is acknowledged, we have still two contrasting forms, and how a novel may now either be Greek in its simplicity, its swiftness, its directness, as the 'Bride of Lammermoor' is, and the 'Scarlet Letter,' and 'Smoke,' with the interest centered in one or two or three characters only; or it may be Elizabethan rather, with a leisurely amplitude, peopled with many characters, such as we see in the 'Heart of Midlothian,' in 'Vanity Fair,' and in 'Anna Karénina.'

The historical study of fiction affords us an opportunity for interesting investigations into what may be called literary genealogy—the inquiry as to the exact value of the inheritance each of the novelists received from his immediate predecessors and as to which particular predecessor it was of whom he is the chief heir. Consciously or unconsciously, every artist is a debtor to the past. The most original of innovators has made his originality partly out of himself, partly out of what he has appropriated and absorbed from those who practised his art before him. Only a few of his separate contrivances are his own, and the most he may claim is a patent on the combination. Now it is not without instruction for us to disentangle the new from the old, and to ascertain whence each of the novelists derived this or that device of which he has made effective use.

Every artist studies in the studio of one or more of his elders, and it is there that he picks up the secrets of his art and receives the precious traditions of the craft. The novice may be absolutely unlike his master; but he must begin by doing what his master tells him to do; and it is only after he has learned his trade that he knows enough to try to develop his own individuality. And so we see how it is that the great Michelangelo was a student under Ghirlandajo, who was not great, and how Botticelli profited by the instruction of Fra Filippo Lippi, who had studied under Masaccio, who had for his master Masolino; and it is instructive for the student of the history of painting to know also that Giulio Romano was the pupil of Raphael, who was the pupil of Perugino, who was the pupil of Nicolò da Foligno, who was the pupil of Benozzo Gozzoli, who was the pupil of Fra Angelico, who although not a pupil was a follower of Giotto, who was a pupil of Cimabue. Thus, and thus only, can the indispensable technic be passed down from generation to generation, every man handing on the accumulation he has received, increasing it by his own contribution. The young artist is a weakling if he openly robs any single one of his predecessors; he is a dolt if he does not borrow from as many of them as may have the separate qualities he is striving to combine.

The arts are one in reality; and what is true of painting and sculpture and architecture is true also of literature—of prose and verse. For example, there are few men of letters of our time whose prose has been more praised for its freshness and its individuality than the late Robert Louis Stevenson; but his was an originality compounded of many simples. He confessed frankly that he had sat at the feet of the masters, playing the "sedulous ape" to a dozen or more, and at last slowly learning how to be himself. Again, the verse of Dante Gabriel Rossetti has a note of its own, a note which many younger poets have delighted to echo and reëcho; but Rossetti told a friend that the exciting cause of his 'Blessed Damozel' was the 'Raven' of Edgar Allan Poe; and Poe's own indebtedness to Coleridge is obvious even if it had not been expressly avowed.

In literature as in life, it is a wise child that knows its own father; and the family-tree of fiction is not easy to trace in all its roots and branches. Certain types persist from one generation to another. We have no hesitation in declaring that the author of the 'Master of Ballantrae' had for his grandfathers in story-telling the author of 'Guy Mannering' and the author of the 'Three Musketeers'; and we may even venture to believe that the young Scotchman who wrote 'Treasure Island' was a literary nephew of the American who wrote the 'Gold Bug' and a great-grandnephew of the Englishman who wrote 'Robinson Crusoe.' Sometimes we can pick out a novelist who is the remote descendant of a series of international marriages. The Italian Signor Gabriele d'Annunzio, for example, came forward first as a writer of fiction with a story which had obviously been inspired by a study of the psychologic subtleties of the Frenchman M. Paul Bourget. But M. Bourget's first novel was obviously modeled upon the delicate work of Mr. Henry James, to whom, indeed, it was dedicated as to a master. Now the earlier tales of the American novelist were plainly written under the influence of a Russian, Ivan Turgenieff. As a whole, Signor d'Annunzio's writings are very different from M. Bourget's, and M. Bourget's from Mr. James's, and Mr. James's from Turgenieff's; but none the less the line of filiation is clearly to be perceived. Of course there is here intended no suggestion of unfair imitation, still less of vulgar plagiarism; the desire is merely to show how each of these accomplished artists in fiction served his apprenticeship in the workshop of an elder craftsman.   In literature there are very few self-made men.

As it happens, these four nineteenth-century novelists have a strong family likeness; they are of kin spiritually; they are all of them far more interested in the subtle workings of the mind of man than in any overt actions of his body.   It would not be difficult, however, to find another group, linked together in like manner, in which there is marked opposition between the successive authors, the younger availing themselves of the technical devices of their masters, but turning these to totally different uses.   For example, no writer of his years has a more vigorous freshness than Mr. Rudyard Kipling; none has shown originality in more diverging lines than he.   Yet Mr. Kipling's first tales from the Indian hills reveal plainly the strong impression left on his youthful genius by the Californian stories of Mr. Bret Harte; and the style at least of Mr. Bret Harte's earlier stories showed how forcibly he had been affected by Charles Dickens. Now Dickens has recorded that his own earlier sketches were deliberately cast in the mold supplied by Smollett in his robust comic portraitures; and Smollett, in the preface of one of his novels, has avowed his emulation of Le Sage. But 'Gil Blas' is an adroit arrangement of material from Spanish sources according to the model set by the authors of 'Lazarillo de Tormes' and 'Guzman de Alfarache,' the original picaresque romances. Between these picaresque romances and 'Gil Blas' and Smollett's full-blooded and coarse-grained fictions there are many points of resemblance; but Dickens, even in the rougher farcical tales of his youth, is not to be classed with them; Mr. Bret Harte's work, as a whole, exhibits no close similarity to Dickens's; and Mr. Rudyard Kipling's, as a whole, exhibits no likeness at all to either Dickens's or Mr. Bret Harte's.

Sometimes the literary ancestry of an author is mixed, and he is not merely a chip of the old block and not quite the image of his father, but has traits inherited from his mother also, and from a dozen other progenitors, maternal and paternal. Mr. Howells is an instance of this felicitous cross-breeding, and he can trace his descent from ancestors as different as Henry Heine and Jane Austen, Turgenieff and Tolstoy. Sometimes an author of our time throws back to a remote forefather; the skeleton of 'Huckleberry Finn,' for example, is loosely articulated like the skeleton of 'Gil Blas,' although Mark Twain once told me, when I drew his attention to this, that he had absolutely no recollection of Le Sage's

story and certainly no predilection for it. The
form here is the picaresque form, which has for
its hero some humble and hopelessly unheroic
figure, before whose wondering eyes more or less
of the strange panorama of life is slowly unrolled.
From ' Gil Blas ' to ' Huckleberry Finn ' the line is
long, running through ' Roderick Random" and the
' Pickwick Papers ' and more than one of Marryat's
happy-go-lucky narratives. Indeed, the laxly
knit tale of this type is likely always to be attractive to the story-teller, as it releases the author
from any obligation to construct a logical plot,
and as it allows him to utilize immediately any
striking situation he may invent or any strange
character he may meet.

III

As the only unity the picaresque romance can
have is due to the fact that a certain character has
been a spectator of the various scenes or an actor
in the various adventures, this character is generally allowed to tell the story himself, and the tale
takes the shape of an autobiography. The autobiography and the history—these are the two
usual methods of communicating to the reader
the events in which his interest is to be aroused;
either one of the characters tells the tale in the
first person or else the author tells it himself in

the third person.   There are other methods, of
course.   The story may be cast in the form of a
diary kept by one of the characters, recording
events from day to day, and revealing in this act
his feelings at the moment of making the entry;
the method of the contemporaneous autobiography, this might be called, and it has been employed skilfully by Mr. Paul Leicester Ford in his
'Story of an Untold Love.'   Or the author may
suppress everything except what his people say
to one another, cutting his story down to dialogue only, with but summary indication either
of actual action or of unexpressed feeling.   This
semi-dramatic method has been developed in
France of late by half a dozen clever writers,
under the lead of the lady who calls herself
"Gyp," and it has been employed by Mr. Rudyard
Kipling in the 'Story of the Gadsbys.'   Or certain
of the characters may exchange letters—which
is a very leisurely way of affording us the information we are seeking.   But this method has
its advantage, if the center of interest is not so
much in what happened as in how these happen-
ings affected the several actors—as in Smollett's
'Humphrey Clinker,' for example, and in Mr.
James's 'Bundle of Letters,' much of the humor
of these pleasantries arising from the unconscious
self-revelation of different characters in the presence of the same fact.   On the other hand, modern

readers find it an immense weariness to be forced to go through all the outlying formulas of epistolary art, when the theme itself is emotion pure and simple—as in Richardson's 'Clarissa Harlowe,' which is to-day left unread partly because of the intolerable sluggishness of its telling. Wilkie Collins found it profitable elaborately to combine letters and diaries and statements of this character and that, thus keeping up an incessant cross-fire of suggestions and suspicions under cover of which the ultimate secret might lie concealed a little longer. Two young friends of mine, in the wantonness of inventive exuberance, once pieced together a coherent story out of race-cards, play-bills, pawn-tickets, newspaper paragraphs, advertisements, telegrams, and a few letters, without a single line of direct narrative. This ingenuity is well enough once in a way, but in the long run there is no doubt that it is worse than wasted. In the art of the story-teller, as in any other art, the less the mere form is flaunted in the eyes of the beholder the better. The simpler the manner of telling the story, the more attention will the reader be able to bestow upon the matter. So we find that the most of the great novels of the world are singularly free from intricacies of composition, and that in them the story is set forth directly either by one of the characters or by the author himself.

Probably the autobiographic form is earlier than
the narrative in the third person.   As Mr. Kipling
once suggested to me when we were discussing
the question, primitive man assumes no modesty, but is frankly vainglorious, rejoicing in his
own prowess and delighting to vaunt himself.
"I did it," he cries, "alone I did it; I seized him,
I smote him, I slew him—with my own right
hand I slew him!"   And even now there is an
almost irresistible tendency to boast when a man
is talking about himself.   Henry Esmond is as
modest as he is manly, but we discover that he
is aware of his own merits.   Barry Lyndon is
outrageously self-laudatory, which does not prevent our perceiving that he is an unmitigated
scoundrel.   In these two masterpieces Thackeray
uses the autobiographic form with perfect success; but when he employs Arthur Pendennis to
unravel for us the family history of the Newcomes, we cannot but think he is less felicitous.
The personality of Pendennis is out of place in
the later story, and his presence is distracting;
besides, we are compelled to ask ourselves more
than once how it is that Pendennis knows all the
secrets of the highly respectable family, and we
do not enjoy the suspicion that he must have
employed detectives or listened at the keyhole.
Nine times out of ten the simplest form is the
best, the plain narrative in the third person by the

author, who is supposed to be ubiquitous and omniscient, having seen everything, heard everything, and remembered everything. The modern novelist, Mr. Howells once reminded me, is the direct heir of the epic poet, who knew all things because he was inspired by the muse herself, her aid having been duly invoked at the beginning. The most accomplished artists in fiction are the French, and they very rarely use any but the plain narrative; and this has been preferred also by Turgenieff in Russia and by Hawthorne in America, with that unerring instinct which makes them the despair of less gifted story-tellers. Turgenieff even managed to endow his plain narrative with some of the advantage of the autobiography, singling out one of his characters, analyzing this one's feelings only, and telling us always how the other characters affected this one.

IV

It may seem to some that I am lingering too long over questions of technic, to which few readers of fiction ever give a thought, being interested in the events of the story, in the people who carry it on, in what is felt and said and done, rather than in the way in which it happens to be told. But a certain understanding of technic is a first requisite for any adequate appreciation of an art; and the technic of the art of the novelist is now singularly rich and varied and worthy of consideration. In our English-speaking community there is no danger that too much attention will be paid to matters of craftsmanship. In art we tend to be slovens, attaining our aim rather by an excessive expenditure of energy than by adroit husbanding of force. The ordinary British novel is a sprawling invertebrate—not to call it an inorganic conglomerate. Even the works of the British masters are often almost amorphous— the 'Mutual Friend' for one and 'Middlemarch' for another, both of which disclose an astounding disregard for the principles of composition. 'Vanity Fair' has two separate stories arbitrarily conjoined—the one recording the rise and fall of Becky Sharp, and the other dealing with the two wooings of Amelia.

When we turn from technic to theme, from the manner of telling to the matter of the tale, there are many aspects of fiction inviting attention, and there are not a few questions of the hour upon which light can be thrown by an examination of the novels of the day. For example, there is incessant discussion about the equality of the sexes and about the difference between feminine and masculine ideals; and here instruction can be had by a comparison of the novels written by men with the novels written by women. Apparently what man most admires in woman is charm and submissiveness; and therefore we discover that heroines of men's novels are likely to be both lovely and insipid, and that they are really clever only when they incline toward wickedness—Amelia on the one hand and on the other Becky Sharp. And seemingly what woman most admires in man is strength and goodness; and therefore we find that the heroes of women's novels tend to be brutes, like Rochester in 'Jane Eyre,' or to be prigs, like Daniel Deronda. Wholly without intention, the writers, men and women both, have disclosed the unformulated and fundamental beliefs of each sex about the other; and the testimony is the stronger from the fact that the witnesses were not aware they were on the stand.

Almost as brisk as this eternal debate between the sexes is the present discussion in regard to race-characteristics, and whether or not, for instance, the civilization of the Anglo-Saxon is really superior to that of the Latin and that of the Slav. Here again fiction may be of invaluable assistance in coming to a wise conclusion. Consider, for example, how the chief qualities of a people are unconsciously disclosed in its novels. Robinson Crusoe is as typically English in his sturdiness and in his religious feeling as the sorrowful Werther is typically German or the light-hearted Manon Lescaut is typically French. Any one who chanced to be familiar with the serious fiction of Spain and America might have forecast the conduct of the recent war between the two countries and foretold the result. Perhaps the salient inconsistency of the Spanish character, the immense chasm between its poetic side and its prosaic, could be seized by the mastery of a single volume, one of the world's greatest books, 'Don Quixote.' But a casual perusal of two earlier stories, 'Lazarillo de Tormes' and 'Guzman de Alfarache,' now nearly three centuries old, would remind us how deeply rooted are certain of the characteristics of the Spanish race—on the one hand empty honor, careless cruelty, besotted superstition, administrative corruption, and on the other sobriety, uncomplaining industry, and cheerful courage. These same characteristics are discoverable also in the later novels of Valdés and Perez Galdos, although not quite so brutally displayed. And as to America, whoever had read and understood the recent serious fiction of the United States, the 'Rise of Silas Lapham' and the 'Hazard of New Fortunes,' the stories of Mr. Hamlin Garland and Mr. Owen Wister, the tales of Miss Wilkins and of "Octave Thanet," might have sized up us Americans, and might have made a pretty good guess at the way

99

a war, once entered upon, would bring out the energy of the race, the tenacity, the resolution, the ingenuity—and even the good-humored and easy-going toleration which is perhaps our chief defect as a people, and which is responsible in some measure for the preventable sufferings of our sick soldiers.

V

I said that a reader of the serious fiction of the two countries might have forecast the result of the war; and by serious fiction I meant what is often called Realistic fiction, the fiction in which the author has tried to tell the truth about life as he sees it. I doubt whether any valid deduction whatever could have been made by a reader of Romanticist fiction, the fiction in which the author feels himself at liberty to dress up the facts of life to suit his market or to delight his caprice. The Romanticist fictions are more exciting than the veritistic; surprise follows surprise, and so-called effects are heaped one on the other. Life as we all know it, with its commonplace duties, seems drear and gray after these excursions into fairy-land with impossible heroes who face impossible perils with impossible fortitude. But story-telling of this sort is as dangerous as any other departure from the truth; and if it "takes us out of ourselves," as the phrase is, if it supplies the "anodyne of dreams," as a British critic calls it, we had best remember that the morphine habit, once acquired, is not readily relinquished.

The purpose of the novel, as of all literature indeed, is partly to amuse, to delight, to relieve. At a certain stage of mental development we are most amused by the unnatural and by the super-natural. As we grow to man's estate we are likely to discover that life itself offers the most interesting outlook to us, and that the fiction which most refreshes us is that which best inter-prets for us life as we know it. The boy in us, it may be,—the boy that survives more or less in every man who ever had a boyhood of his own, —the boy in us has a boyish liking still for deeds of daring and for swift sequences of hairbreadth escapes; but such puerilities pall sooner or later after a man has once plumbed the depths of life and seen for himself its seriousness. "When I was a child, I spake as a child," said the apostle, "I understood as a child, I thought as a child: but when I became a man, I put away childish things." And the skeptic Montaigne tells us in his essay on books how he outgrew his youthful fondness for the marvelous. "As to the Ama-dises, and such kind of stuff, they had not the credit to take me so much as in my childhood. And I will moreover say (whether boldly or rashly)

101

that this old heavy soul of mine is now no longer
delighted with Ariosto, no, nor with the good fellow Ovid; his facility and invention, with which
I was formerly so ravished, are now of no relish, and I can hardly have the patience to read
him." If Montaigne felt thus three hundred years
ago, before the birth of the modern novel, we
may perhaps maintain now that a continued preference for narratives of physical excitement is a
sign of mental immaturity.

Montaigne could see only the first of the four
stages through which fiction has been developed,
and the fourth of them has been evolved only in
our own time. Fiction dealt first with the Impossible, then with the Improbable, next with
the Probable, and now at last with the Inevitable.
The romances of chivalry, the ' Amadis of Gaul,'
and its sequels, of which Montaigne wearied, may
serve as a type of the first stage, abounding as
they do in deeds frankly impossible; and it is
not unfair to find specimens of the second class
in the Waverley Novels, in the Leatherstocking
Tales, and in the cycle of the Three Musketeers,
wherein we are entranced by adventures, perhaps
always possible but often highly improbable. In
the third group come the gentle novels of Jane
Austen, confining themselves wholly to things
probable; and in the final division we have Turgenieff, for example, handling the common stuff

of humanity, the plain matters of daily life, so as to bring out the inevitable result of the action and reaction of circumstance and character.

Sir Walter Scott once quoted the lumbering and inadequate definitions by means of which Dr. Johnson sought to differentiate the romance and the novel. A romance, in Dr. Johnson's eyes, was "a military fable of the Middle Ages, a tale of wild adventure in love and chivalry," while a novel was "a smooth tale, generally of love." Scott himself proposed to amend by defining a romance as "a fictitious narrative in prose or verse, the interest of which turns upon marvelous or uncommon incidents," and a novel as "a fictitious narrative, differing from the romance because the events are accommodated to the ordinary train of human events and the modern state of society." With his usual clear-headed common sense Scott seized the true line of demarcation, and his definition holds to-day, although the novel has expanded immensely of late and has aspects now that would greatly have surprised him. The novel takes for its own what is likely, what is usual, what is ordinary, while the romance revels in the unlikely, the unusual, and the extraordinary. The novel could not come into existence until after fiction had progressed from the Impossible and the Improbable at least to the Probable. To this day the romance seems to many a mere amusement, the sport of an idle hour, and therefore none too respectable; whereas the novel is held to a higher responsibility, and since it aspires to the dignity of the drama it must be judged by the same lofty standards.

Romance is fond of trying to improve its literary standing by pretending that it is also history. It was John Richard Green who once defined a novel as " history without documents—nothing to prove it"; and it is possible that the historian of the English people meant by this to exclude that bastard hybrid of fact and fancy which is known as the historical romance. We recognize that the tales of Russian life, for instance, which traveling Frenchmen have narrated, cannot be wholly trustworthy, or at least we can guess at their inexactness by recalling the stories of America written by British authors; and we cannot deny that the author of a historical romance is also a carpet-bagger,—not through space, but through time,—and if his blunders be not so obvious, none the less must he blunder abundantly. As the best novels of Russian life are those written by the Russians themselves and the best novels of American life are those written by Americans, so the best novels of eighteenth-century manners, for example, are those written in the eighteenth century, and the most adequate stories of the Italian Renascence are the stories written by Italians during the Renascence. If 'Romola' is a great book, it is great not because of its historical pretensions, but in spite of them. The historical romances of writers less well equipped than George Eliot need detain the student of fiction but very briefly.

VI

A consideration of the history of the modern novel brings out two facts: first, that the technic has been steadily improving, that the story is now told more directly, that character is now portrayed more carefully and elaborately, and that the artist is more self-respecting and takes his work more seriously; and, second, that the desire to reproduce life with all its intricacies has increased with the ability to accomplish this. The best fiction of the nineteenth century is far less artificial and less arbitrary than the best fiction of the eighteenth century. Serious novelists now seek for the interest of their narratives not in the accidents that befall the hero, nor in the external perils from which he chances to escape, but rather in the man himself, in his character with its balance of good and evil, in his struggle with his conscience, in his reaction against his heredity and his environment. Know thyself, said the Greek philosopher, and the English poet told us that the proper study of mankind is man. The modern novel, wisely studied, is an instrument of great subtlety for the acquiring of a knowledge of ourselves and of our fellow-men. It broadens our sympathy by telling us how the other half lives, and it also sharpens our insight into humanity at large. It helps us to take a large and liberal view of life; it enlightens, it sustains, and it cheers. What Mr. John Morley once said of literature as a whole is even more accurate when applied to fiction alone: its purpose is " to bring sunshine into our hearts and to drive moonshine out of our heads."

(1898)

V

ALPHONSE DAUDET

[This biographical criticism was written to serve as an Introduction to the translation of Daudet's works issued by Messrs. Little, Brown & Co.]

ALPHONSE DAUDET

ALPHONSE DAUDET is one of the most richly gifted of modern French novelists and one of the most artistic; he is perhaps the most delightful, and he is certainly the most fortunate. In his own country earlier than any of his contemporaries he saw his stories attain to the very wide circulation that brings both celebrity and wealth. Beyond the borders of his own language he swiftly won a popularity both with the broad public and with the professed critics of literature second only to that of Victor Hugo and still surpassing that of Balzac, who is only of late beginning to receive from us the attention he has so long deserved.

Daudet has had the rare luck of pleasing partizans of almost every school; the Realists have joyed in his work and so have the Romanticists; his writings have found favor in the eyes of the frank Impressionists and also at the hands of the severer custodians of academic standards. Mr. Henry James has declared that Daudet is "at the head of his profession," and has called him " an admirable genius." Mr. Robert Louis Stevenson thought Daudet "incomparably" the best of the present French novelists, and asserted that ' Kings in Exile' comes " very near to being a master-piece." M. Jules Lemaitre tells us that Daudet "trails all hearts after him — because he has charm, as indefinable in a work of art as in a woman's face." M. Ferdinand Brunetière, who has scant relish for latter-day methods in lit-erature, admits ungrudgingly that "there are certain corners of the great city and certain as-pects of Parisian manners, there are some physi-ognomies that perhaps no one has been able to render so well as Daudet, with that infinitely subtle and patient art which succeeds in giving even to inanimate things the appearance of life."

I

The documents are abundant for an analysis of Daudet such as Sainte-Beuve would have under-taken with avidity; they are more abundant, indeed, than for any other contemporary French man of letters even in these days of unhesitating self-revelation; and they are also of an absolutely impregnable authenticity. M. Ernest Daudet has written a whole volume to tell us all about his brother's boyhood and youth and early manhood and first steps in literature. M. Léon Daudet has written another solid tome to tell us all about his father's literary principles and family life and later years and death. Daudet himself put forth a pair of pleasant books of personal gossip about himself, narrating his relations with his fellow-authors, and recording the circumstances under which he came to compose each of his earlier stories. Montaigne — whose 'Essays' was Daudet's bedside book, and who may be accepted not unfairly as an authority upon egotism — assures us that "there is no description so difficult, nor doubtless of so great utility, as that of one's self." And Daudet's own interest in himself is not unlike Montaigne's — it is open, innocent, and illuminating.

Cuvier may have been able to reconstruct an extinct monster from the inspection of a single bone; but it is a harder task to revive the figure of a man, even by the aid of these family testimonies, this self-analysis, the diligence of countless interviewers of all nationalities, and the indiscretion of a friend like Édmond de Goncourt (who seems to have acted on the theory that it is the whole duty of man to take notes of the talk of his fellows for prompt publication). Yet we have ample material to enable us to trace Daudet's heredity, and to estimate the influence of his environment in the days of his youth, and to allow for the effect which certain of his own physical peculiarities must have had upon his exercise of his art. His near-sightedness, for example — would not Sainte-Beuve have seized upon this as significant? Would he not have seen in this a possible source of Daudet's mastery of description? And the spasms of pain borne bravely and uncomplainingly, the long agony of his later years, what mark has this left on his work, how far is it responsible for a modification of his attitude — for the change from the careless gaiety of 'Tartarin of Tarascon' to the somber satire of 'Port Tarascon'? What caused the joyous story-teller of the 'Letters from my Mill' to develop into the bitter iconoclast of the 'Immortal'?

These questions are insistent; and yet, after all, what matters the answer to any of them? The fact remains that Daudet had his share of that incommunicable quality which we are agreed to call genius. This once admitted, we may do our best to weigh it and to resolve it into its elements; it is at bottom the vital spark that resists all examination, however scientific we may seek to be. We can test for this and for that, but in the final analysis genius is inexplicable. It is what it is because it is. It might have been different, no doubt, but it is not. It is its own excuse for being; and, for all that we can say to the contrary, it is its own cause, sufficient unto itself. Even if we had Sainte-Beuve's scalpel, we could not surprise the secret.

Yet an inquiry into the successive stages of Daudet's career, a consideration of his ancestry, of his parentage, of his birth, of the circumstances of his boyhood, of his youthful adventures — these things are interesting in themselves, and they are not without instruction. They reveal to us the reasons for the transformation that goes so far to explain Daudet's peculiar position — the transformation of a young Provençal poet into a brilliant Parisian veritist. Daudet was a Provençal who became a Parisian; and in this translation we may find the key to his character as a writer of fiction.

He was from Provence as Maupassant was from Normandy; and Daudet had the Southern expansiveness and abundance, just as Maupassant had the Northern reserve and caution. If an author is ever to bring forth fruit after his kind he must have roots in the soil of his nativity. Daudet was no orchid, beautiful and scentless; his writings have always the full flavor of the Southern soil. He was able to set Tartarin before us so sympathetically and to make Numa Roumestan so convincing because he recognized in himself the possibility of a like exuberance. He could never take the rigorously impassive

attitude which Flaubert taught Maupassant to
assume. Daudet not only feels for his characters,
but he is quite willing that we should be aware
of his compassion.

He is not only incapable of the girding enmity
which Taine detected and detested in Thackeray's
treatment of Becky Sharp, but he is also devoid
of the callous detachment with which Flaubert
dissected Emma Bovary under the microscope.
Daudet is never flagrantly hostile toward one of
his creatures; and however contemptible or des-
picable the characters he has called into being,
he is scrupulously fair to them. Sidonie and Félicia Ruys severally throw themselves away, but
Daudet is never intolerant. He is inexorable,
but he is not insulting. I cannot but think that
it is Provence whence Daudet derived the precious
birthright of sympathy, and that it is Provence
again which bestowed on him the rarer gift of
sentiment. It is by his possession of sympathy
and of sentiment that he has escaped the arid-
ity which suffocates us in the works of so many
other Parisian novelists. The South endowed
him with warmth and heartiness and vivacity;
and what he learned from Paris was the power of
self-restraint and the duty of finish.

He was born in Provence and he died in Paris;
he began as a poet and he ended as a veritist;
and in each case there was logical evolution and

not contradiction.   The Parisian did not cease to
be a Provençal; and the novelist was a lyrist still.
Poet though he was, he had an intense liking for
the actual, the visible, the tangible.   He so hun-
gered after truth that he was ready sometimes to
stay his stomach with facts in its stead — mere
fact being but the outward husk, whereas truth
is the rich kernel concealed within.   His son tells
us that Daudet might have taken as a motto the
title of Goethe's autobiography, 'Dichtung und
Wahrheit' — 'Poetry and Truth.'   And this it is
that has set Daudet apart and that has caused his
vogue with readers of all sorts and conditions
— this unique combination of imagination and
verity.   "His originality," M. Jules Lemaitre has
acutely remarked, "is closely to unite observation and fantasy, to extract from the truth all
that it contains of the improbable and the surprising, to satisfy at the same time the readers
of M. Cherbuliez and the readers of M. Zola, to
write novels which are at the same time Realistic
and Romantic, and which seem Romantic only
because they are very sincerely and very profoundly Realistic."

II

Alphonse Daudet was born in 1840, and it was
at Nîmes that he first began to observe mankind;
and he has described his birthplace and his boyhood

in 'Little What's-his-name,' a novel even richer in autobiographical revelation than is 'David Copperfield.' His father was a manufacturer whose business was not prosperous and who was forced at last to remove with the whole family to Lyons in the vain hope of doing better in the larger town. After reading the account of this parent's peculiarities in M. Ernest Daudet's book, we are not surprised that the affairs of the family did not improve, but went from bad to worse. Alphonse Daudet suffered bitterly in these years of desperate struggle, but he gained an understanding of the conditions of mercantile life to be serviceable later in the composition of 'Fromont and Risler.'

When he was sixteen he secured a place as *pion* in a boarding-school in the Cévennes. A pion is a poor devil of a youth hired to keep watch on the boys. How painful this position was to the young poet can be read indirectly in 'Little What's-his-name,' but more explicitly in the history of that story, printed now in 'Thirty Years of Paris.' From this remote prison he was rescued by his elder brother, Ernest, who was trying to make his way in Paris, and who sent for Alphonse as soon as he had been engaged to help an old gentleman in writing his memoirs. The younger brother has described his arrival in Paris, and his first dress-coat, and his earliest literary acquaintances. Ernest's salary was seventy-five francs a month, and on this the two brothers managed to live; no doubt fifteen dollars went further in Paris in 1857 than they did forty years later.

In those days of privation and ambition Daudet's longing was to make himself famous as a poet; and when at last, not yet twenty years old, he began his career as a man of letters, it was by the publication of a volume of verse, just as his fellow-novelists, M. Paul Bourget and Signor Gabriele d'Annunzio have severally done. Immature as juvenile lyrics are likely to be, these early rimes of Daudet's have a flavor of their own, a faintly recognizable note of individuality. He is more naturally a poet than most modern literators who possess the accomplishment of verse as part of their equipment for the literary life, but who lack a spontaneous impulse toward rhythm. It may even be suggested that his little poems are less artificial than most French verse; they are the result of a less obvious effort. He lisped in numbers; and with him it was rather prose that had to be consciously acquired. His lyric note, although not keen and not deep, is heard again and again in his novels, and it sustains some of the most graceful and tender of his short-stories — the 'Death of the Dauphin,' for instance, and the 'Sous-préfet in the Fields.'

Daudet extended poetry to include playmaking; and alone or with a friend he attempted more than one little piece in rime — tiny plays of a type familiar enough at the Odéon. He has told us how the news of the production of one of these poetic dramas came to him afar in Algiers, whither he had been sent because of a weakness of the lungs, threatening to become worse in the gray Parisian winter. Other plays of his, some of them far more important than this early effort, were produced in the next few years. The most ambitious of these was the 'Woman of Arles,' which he had elaborated from a touching short-story, and for which Bizet composed incidental music as beautiful and as overwhelming as that prepared by Mendelssohn for the 'Midsummer Night's Dream.'

No one of Daudet's dramatic attempts was really successful — not the 'Woman of Arles,' which is less moving in the theater than in its briefer narrative form, not even the latest of them all, the freshest and the most vigorous, the 'Struggle for Life,' with its sinister figure of Paul Astier taken over from the 'Immortal.' Apparently, with all his desire to write for the stage, Daudet must have been inadequately endowed with the dramaturgic faculty, that special gift of playmaking which many a poet lacks and many a novelist, but which the humblest playwright

must needs have and which all the great dramatists have possessed abundantly in addition to
their poetic power.

Perhaps it was the unfavorable reception of his
successive dramas which is responsible for the
chief of Daudet's lapses from the kindliness with
which he treats the characters that people his
stories. He seems to have kept hot a grudge
against the theater, and he relieves his feelings
by taking it out of the stage-folk he introduces
into his novels. To actors and actresses he is
intolerant and harsh. What is factitious and
self-overvaluing in the Provençal type, he understood and he found it easy to pardon; but
what was factitious and self-overvaluing in the
player type, he would not understand and he
refused to pardon. And here he shows in strong
contrast with a successful dramatist, M. Ludovic
Halévy, whose knowledge of the histrionic temperament is at least as wide as Daudet's and
whose humor is as keen, but whose judgment
is softened by the grateful memory of many vic-
tories won by the united effort of the author and
the actor.

Through his brother's influence, Alphonse
Daudet was appointed by the Duke of Morny to
a semi-sinecure; and he has recorded how he
told his benefactor before accepting the place that
he was a Legitimist, and how the Duke smilingly

retorted that the Empress was also. Although it was as a poet that Daudet made his bow in the world of letters, his first appearance as a dramatist was not long delayed thereafter; and he soon came forward also as a journalist — or rather as a contributor to the papers. While many of the articles he prepared for the daily and weekly press were of ephemeral interest only, as the necessity of journalism demands, to be forgotten forty-eight hours after they were printed, not a few of them were sketches having more than a temporary value. Parisian newspapers are more hospitable to literature than are the newspapers of New York or of London, and a goodly proportion of the young Southerner's journalistic writing proved worthy of preservation.

It has been preserved for us in three volumes of short-stories and sketches, of fantasies and impressions. Not all the contents of the 'Letters from my Mill,' of the 'Monday Tales,' and of 'Artists' Wives,' as we have these collections now, were written in these early years of Daudet's Parisian career, but many of them saw the light before 1870, and what has been added since conforms in method to the work of his prentice days. No doubt the war with Prussia enlarged his outlook on life; and there is more depth in the satires this conflict suggested and more pathos in the pictures it evoked. The 'Last Lesson,' for example, that simple vision of the old French schoolmaster taking leave of his Alsatian pupils, has a symbolic breath not easy to match in the livelier tales written before the surrender at Sedan; and in the 'Siege of Berlin' there is a vibrant patriotism far more poignant than we can discover in any of the playful apologues published before the war. He had had an inside view of the Second Empire; he could not help seeing its hollowness, and he revolted against the selfishness of its servants; no single chapter of M. Zola's splendid and terrible 'Downfall' contains a more damning indictment of the leaders of the imperial army than is to be read in Daudet's 'Game of Billiards.'

The short-story, whether in prose or in verse, is a literary form in which the French have ever displayed an easy mastery; and from Daudet's three volumes it would not be difficult to select half a dozen little masterpieces. The Provençal tales lack only rimes to stand confessed as poesy; and many a reader may prefer these first flights, before Daudet set his Pegasus to toil in the mill of realism. The 'Pope's Mule,' for instance, is not this a marvel of blended humor and fantasy? And the 'Elixir of Father Gaucher,' what could be more naïvely ironic? Like a true Southerner, Daudet delights in girding at the church; and these tales bristle with gibes at ecclesiastical dignitaries; but his stroke is never malignant, and there is no barb to his shaft nor poison on the tip.

Scarcely inferior to the war stories or to the Provençal sketches are certain vignettes of the capital, swift silhouettes of Paris, glimpsed by an unforgetting eye — the 'Last Book,' for one, in which an unlovely character is treated with kindly contempt; and for another, the 'Book-keeper,' the most Dickens-like of Daudet's shorter pieces, yet having a literary modesty Dickens never attained. The alleged imitation of the British novelist by the French may be left for later consideration; but it is possible now to note that in the earlier descriptive chapters of the 'Letters from my Mill' one may detect a certain similarity of treatment and attitude, not to Dickens but to two of the masters on whom Dickens modeled himself—Goldsmith and Irving. The scene in the diligence, when the baker gently pokes fun at the poor fellow whose wife is intermittent in her fidelity, is quite in the manner of the 'Sketch-Book.'

There is the same freshness and fertility in the collection called 'Artists' Wives' as in the 'Letters from my Mill' and the 'Monday Tales,' but not the same playfulness and fun. They are severe studies, all of them; and they all illustrate

the truth of Bagehot's saying that a man's mother
might be his misfortune, but his wife was his fault.
It is a rosary of marital infelicities that Daudet
has strung for us in this volume, and in every
one of them the husband is expiating his blunder.
With ingenious variety the author rings the
changes on one theme, on the sufferings of the
ill-mated poet or painter or sculptor, despoiled
of the sympathy he craves, and shackled even in
the exercise of his art. And the picture is not
out of drawing, for Daudet can see the wife's
side of the case also; he can appreciate her be-
wilderment at the ugly duckling whom it is so
difficult for her to keep in the nest. The women
have made shipwreck of their lives too, and they
are companions in misery, if not helpmeets in
understanding. This is perhaps the saddest of
all Daudet's books, the least relieved by humor,
the most devoid of the gaiety which illumines
the 'Letters from my Mill' and the first and
second Tartarin volumes. But it is also one
of the most veracious; it is life itself firmly
grasped and honestly presented.

It is not matrimonial incongruity at large in all
its shifting aspects that Daudet here considers;
it is only the married unhappiness of the artist,
whatever his mode of expression and whichever of the muses he has chosen to serve; it is
only the wedded life of the man incessantly in

search of the ideal, and never relaxing in the strain of his struggle with the inflexible material from which he must shape his vision of existence. Not only in this book but in many another has Daudet shown that he perceives the needs of the artistic temperament, its demands, its limitations, and its characteristics. There is a playwright in 'Rose and Ninette'; there is a painter in the 'Immortal'; there is an actor in 'Fromont and Risler'; there are a sculptor, a poet, and a novelist on the roll of the heroine's lovers in 'Sapho.' Daudet handles them gently always, unless they happen to belong to the theater. Toward the stage-folk he is pitiless; for all other artists he has abundant appreciation; he is not blind to their little weaknesses, but these he can forgive even though he refuses to forget; he is at home with them. He is never patronizing, as Thackeray is, who also knows them and loves them. Thackeray's attitude is that of a gentleman born to good society, but glad to visit Bohemia, because he can speak the language; Daudet's is that of a man of letters who thinks that his fellow-artists are really the best society.

III

Not with pictures of artists at home did Daudet conquer his commanding position in literature, not with short-stories, not with plays, not with verses. These had served to make him known to the inner circle of lovers of literature who are quick to appreciate whatever is at once new and true; but they did not help him to break through the crust and to reach the hearts of the broad body of readers who care little for the delicacies of the season, but must ever be fed on strong meat. When the latest of the three volumes of short-stories was published, and when the 'Woman of Arles' was produced, the transformation was complete: the poet had developed into a veritist without ceasing to be a poet, and the Provençal had become a Parisian. His wander-years were at an end, and he had made a happy marriage. Lucky in the risky adventure of matrimony, as in so many others, he chanced upon a woman who was congenial, intelligent, and devoted, and who became almost a collaborator in all his subsequent works.

His art was ready for a larger effort; it was ripe for a richer fruitage. Already had he made more than one attempt at a long story, but this was before his powers had matured and before he had come to a full knowledge of himself. 'Little What's-his-name,' as he himself has confessed, lacks perspective; it was composed too soon after the personal experiences out of which it was made — before time had put the scenes in proper proportion and before his hand was firm in its stroke. 'Robert Helmont' is the journal of an observer who happens also to be a poet and a patriot; but it has scarcely substance enough to warrant calling it a story. Much of the material used in the making of these books was very good indeed; but the handling was a little uncertain, and the result is not quite satisfactory, charming as both of them are, with the seductive grace which is Daudet's birthright and his trade-mark. In his brief tales he had shown that he had the story-telling faculty, the ability to project character, the gift of arousing interest; but it remained for him to prove that he possessed also the main strength requisite to carry him through the long labor of a full-grown novel. It is not by gentle stories like 'Robert Helmont' and 'Little What's-his-name' that a novelist is promoted to the front rank; and after he had written these two books he remained where he was before, in the position of a promising young author.

The promise was fulfilled by the publication of 'Fromont and Risler'—not the best of his novels, but the earliest in which his full force was displayed. Daudet has told us how this was planned originally as a play, how the failure of the 'Woman of Arles' led him to relinquish the dramatic form, and how the supposed necessities of the stage warped the logical structure of the story, wrenching to the intrigues of the young wife the interest which should have been concentrated upon the partnership, the business rivalry, the mercantile integrity, whence the novel derived its novelty. Daudet yielded only this once to the falsifying habit of thrusting marital infidelity into the foreground of fiction when the theme itself seems almost to exclude any dwelling on amorous misadventure; and this is one reason why a truer view of Parisian life can be found in his pages than in those of any of his competitors, and why his works are far less monotonous than theirs.

He is not squeamish, as every reader of 'Sapho' can bear witness; but he does not wantonly choose a vulgar adultery as the staple of his stories. French fiction, ever since the tale of 'Tristan and Yseult' was first told, has tended to be a poem of love triumphant over every obstacle, even over honor; and Daudet is a Frenchman, with French ideas about woman and love and marriage. He is not without his share of Gallic salt; but he is too keen an observer not to see that there are other things in life than illicit wooings — business, for example, and politics, and religion — important factors all of them in our complicated modern existence. At the root of him Daudet had a steadfast desire to see life as a whole and to tell the truth about it unhesitatingly; and this is a characteristic he shares only with the great masters of fiction — essentially veracious, every one of them.

Probably Dickens, frequently as he contorted the facts of life into conformity with his rather primitive artistic code, believed that he also was telling the truth. It is in Daudet's paper explaining how he came to write 'Fromont and Risler' that he discusses the accusation that he was an imitator of Dickens — an accusation which seems absurd enough now that the careers of both writers are closed, and that we can compare their complete works. Daudet records that the charge was brought against him very early, long before he had read Dickens, and he explains that any likeness that may exist is due not to copying but to kinship of spirit. "I have deep in my heart," he says, "the same love Dickens has for the maimed and the poor, for the children brought up in all the deprivation of great cities." This pity for the disinherited, for those that have had no chance in life, is not the only similarity between the British novelist and the French; there is also the peculiar combination of sentiment and humor. Daudet is not so overmastering as Dickens; but he is far more discreet, far truer to nature, far finer in his art; he does not let his humor carry him into caricature, nor his sentiment weaken into sentimentality.

Even the minor French novelists strive for beauty of form, and would be ashamed of the fortuitous scaffolding that satisfies the British story-tellers. A eulogist of Dickens, Mr. George Gissing, has recently remarked acutely that "Daudet has a great advantage in his mastery of construction. Where, as in 'Fromont and Risler,' he constructs too well, that is to say, on the stage model, we see what a gain it was to him to have before his eyes the Paris stage of the Second Empire, instead of that of London in the earlier Victorian time." Where Dickens emulated the farces and the melodramas of forgotten British playwrights, Daudet was influenced rather by the virile dramas of Dumas *fils* and Augier. But in 'Fromont and Risler,' not only is the plot a trifle stagy, but the heroine herself seems almost a refugee from the footlights. Exquisitely presented as Sidonie is, she fails quite to captivate or convince, perhaps because her sisters have been seen so often before in this play and in that. And now and again even in his later novels we discover that Daudet has needlessly achieved the adroit arrangement of events so useful in the theater and not requisite in the library. In the 'Nabob,' for example, it is the "long arm of coincidence" that brings Paul de Géry to the inn on the Riviera, and to the very next room therein at the exact moment

when Jenkins catches up with the fleeing
Félicia.

Yet these lapses into the arbitrary are infrequent after all; and as 'Fromont and Risler' was
followed first by one and then by another novel,
the evil influence of theatrical conventionalism
disappears. Daudet occasionally permits himself an underplot; but he acted always on the
principle he once formulated to his son: "Every
book is an organism; if it has not its organs in
place, it dies, and its corpse is a scandal." Sometimes, as in 'Fromont and Risler,' he starts at
the moment when the plot thickens, returning
soon to make clear the antecedents of the characters first shown in action; and sometimes, as
in 'Sapho,' he begins right at the beginning and
goes straight through to the end. But, whatever
his method, there is never any doubt as to the
theme; and the essential unity is always apparent.
This severity of design in no way limits the variety of the successive acts of his drama.

While a novel of Balzac's is often no more than
an analysis of character, and while a novel of
Zola's is a massive epic of human endeavor, a
novel of Daudet's is a gallery of pictures, brushed
in with the sweep and certainty of a master
hand — portraits, landscapes with figures, ma-
rines, battle-pieces, bits of genre, views of Paris.
And the views of Paris outnumber the others,

and almost outvalue them also. Mr. Henry
James has noted that the 'Nabob' is "full of
episodes which are above all pages of execution,
triumphs of translation. The author has drawn
up a list of the Parisian solemnities, and painted
the portrait or given a summary of each of them.
The opening day at the Salon, a funeral at Père
la Chaise, a debate in the Chamber of Deputies,
the *première* of a new play at a favorite theater,
furnish him with so many opportunities for his
gymnastics of observation." And the 'Nabob'
is only a little more richly decorated than the
'Immortal,' and 'Numa Roumestan,' and 'Kings
in Exile.'

These pictures, these carefully wrought masterpieces of rendering, are not lugged in, each for
its own sake; they are not outside of the narrative; they are actually part of the substance of
the story. Daudet excels in describing, and
every artist is prone to abound in the sense of
his superiority. As the French saying puts it, a
man has always the defects of his qualities. Yet
Daudet rarely obtrudes his descriptions, and he
generally uses them to explain character and to
set off or bring out the moods of his personages.
They are so swift that I am tempted to call them
flash-lights; but photographic is just what they
are not, for they are artistic in their vigorous suppression of unessentials; they are never gray or

cold or hard; they vibrate with color and tingle with emotion.

And just as a painter keeps filling his sketch-books with graphic hints for elaboration later, so Daudet was indefatigable in note-taking. He explains his method in his paper of 'Fromont and Risler': how he had for a score of years made a practice of jotting down in little note-books not only his remarks and his thoughts, but also a rapid record of what he had heard with his ears ever on the alert, and what he had seen with those tireless eyes of his. Yet he never let the dust of these note-books choke the life out of him. Every one of his novels was founded on fact — plot, incidents, characters, and scenery.

He used his imagination to help him to see; he used it also to peer into and behind the mere facts. All that he needed to invent was a connecting link now and again; and it may as well be admitted at once that these mere inventions are sometimes the least satisfactory part of his stories. The two young men in the 'Nabob,' for instance, whom Mr. Henry James found it difficult to tell apart, the sculptor-painter in the 'Immortal,' the occasional other characters which we discover to be made up, lack the individuality and the vitality of figures taken from real life by a sympathetic effort of interpretative imagination. Delobelle, Gardinois, ''all the personages of

'Fromont' have lived," Daudet declares; and he adds a regret that in depicting old Gardinois he gave pain to one he loved, but he "could not suppress this type of egotist, aged and terrible."

Since the beginning of the art of story-telling, the narrators must have gone to actuality to get suggestions for their character-drawing; and nothing is commoner than the accusation that this or that novelist has stolen his characters ready-made — filching them from nature's shop-window, without so much as a by-your-leave. Daudet is bold in committing these larcenies from life, and frank in confessing them — far franker than Dickens, who tried to squirm out of the charge that he had put Landor and Leigh Hunt unfairly into fiction. Perhaps Dickens was bolder than Daudet, if it is true that he drew Micawber from his own father, and Mrs. Nickleby from his own mother. Daudet was taxed with ingratitude that he had used as the model of Mora the Duke of Morny, who had befriended him; and he defended himself by declaring that he thought the Duke would find no fault with the way Mora had been presented. But a great artist has never copied his models slavishly; he has utilized them in the effort to realize to his own satisfaction what he has already imagined. Daudet maintained to his son that those who are without imagination cannot even observe accurately. In-

vention alone, mere invention, an inferior form of
mental exercise, suffices to provide a pretty fair
Romanticist tale, remote from the facts of every-
day life; but only true imagination can sustain a
Realistic novel, where every reader's experience
qualifies him to check off the author's progress,
step by step.

IV

It would take too long — although the task
would be amusing — to call the roll of Daudet's
novels written after 'Fromont and Risler' had
revealed to him his own powers, and to discuss
what fact of Parisian history had been the start-
ing-point of each of them, and what notabilities
of Paris had sat for each of the chief characters.
Mr. Henry James, for instance, has seen it suggested that Félicia Ruys is intended as a portrait
of Mme. Sarah Bernhardt; M. Zola, on the other
hand, denies that Félicia Ruys is Mme. Sarah
Bernhardt, and hints that she is rather Mme.
Judith Gautier. Daudet himself refers to the
equally absurd report that Gambetta was the original of Numa Roumestan — a report over which
the alleged subject and the real author laughed
together. Daudet's own attitude toward his
creations is a little ambiguous or at least a little
inconsistent; in one paper he asserts that every
character of his has had a living original, and in

another he admits that Élysée Méraut, for example, is only in part a certain Thérion.

The admission is more nearly exact than the assertion. Every novelist whose work is to endure even for a generation must draw from life, sometimes generalizing broadly and sometimes keeping close to the single individual, but always free to modify the mere fact as he may have observed it to conform with the larger truth of the fable he shall devise. Most story-tellers tend to generalize, and their fictions lack the sharpness of outline we find in nature. Daudet preferred to retain as much of the actual individual as he dared without endangering the web of his composition; and often the transformation is very slight—Mora, for instance, who is probably a close copy of Morny, but who stands on his own feet in the 'Nabob,' and lives his own life as independently as though he was a sheer imagination. More rarely the result is not so satisfactory—J. Tom Lévis, for example, for whose authenticity the author vouches, but who seems out of place in 'Kings in Exile,' like a fantastic invention, such as Balzac sometimes permitted himself as a relief from his rigorous realism.

For incident as well as for character Daudet goes to real life. The escape of Colette from under the eyes of her father-in-law — that actually happened, but none the less does it fit into

'Kings in Exile'; and Colette's cutting off her hair in grief at her husband's death—that actually happened also ; but it belongs artistically in the 'Immortal.' On the other hand, the fact which served as the foundation of the 'Immortal'—the taking in of a savant by a lot of forged manuscripts—has been falsified by changing the savant from a mathematician (who might easily be deceived about a matter of autographs) to a historian (whose duty it is to apply all known tests of genuineness to papers purporting to shed new light on the past). This borrowing from the newspapers has its evident advantages, but it has its dangers also, even in the hands of a poet as adroit as Daudet and as imaginative. Perhaps the story of his which is most artistic in its telling, most shapely, most harmonious in its modulations of a single theme to the inevitable end, developed without haste and without rest, is 'Sapho'; and 'Sapho' is the novel of Daudet's in which there seems to be the least of this stenciling of actual fact, in which the generalization is the broadest, and in which the observation is least restricted to single individuals.

But in 'Sapho' the theme itself is narrow, narrower than in 'Numa Roumestan,' and far narrower than in either the 'Nabob' or 'Kings in Exile'; and this is why 'Sapho,' fine as it is, and subtle, is perhaps less satisfactory. No other

French novelist of the final half of the nineteenth century, not Flaubert, not Goncourt, not M. Zola, not Maupassant, has four novels as solid as these, as varied in incident, as full of life, as rich in character, as true. They form the quadrilateral wherein Daudet's fame is secure.

'Sapho' is a daughter of the 'Lady of the Camellias,' and a granddaughter of 'Manon Lescaut'—Frenchwomen, all of them, and of a class French authors have greatly affected. But Daudet's book is not a specimen of what Lowell called "that *corps-de-ballet* literature in which the most animal of the passions is made more temptingly naked by a veil of French gauze." It is at bottom a moral book, much as 'Tom Jones' is moral. Fielding's novel is English, robust, hearty, brutal in a way, and its morality is none too lofty. Daudet's is French, softer, more enervating, and with an almost complacent dwelling on the sins of the flesh. But neither Fielding nor Daudet is guilty of sentimentality, the one unforgivable crime in art. In his treatment of the relation of the sexes Daudet was above all things truthful; his veracity is inexorable. He shows how man is selfish in love and woman also, and how the egotism of the one is not as the egotism of the other. He shows how Fanny Legrand slangs her lover with the foul language of the gutter whence she sprang, and how Jean, when he strikes back, refrains from foul blows. He shows how Jean, weak of will as he was, gets rid of the millstone about his neck, only because of the weariness of the woman to whom he has bound himself. He shows us the various aspects of the love which is not founded on esteem, the Héttema couple, De Potter and Rose, Déchelette and Alice Doré, all to set off the sorry idyl of Fanny and Jean.

In 'Numa Roumestan' there is a larger vision of life than in 'Sapho,' even if there is no deeper insight. The construction is almost as severe; and the movement is unbroken from beginning to end, without excursus or digression. The central figure is masterly — the kindly and selfish Southerner, easy-going and soft-spoken, an orator who is so eloquent that he can convince even himself, a politician who thinks only when he is talking, a husband who loves his wife as profoundly as he can love anybody except himself, and who loves his wife more than his temporary mistress, even during the days of his dalliance. Numa is a native of the South of France, as was Daudet himself; and it is out of the fulness of knowledge that the author evolves the character, brushing in the portrait with bold strokes and unceasingly adding caressing touches till the man actually lives and moves before our eyes. The veracity of the picture is destroyed by no final

inconsistency. What Numa is, Numa will be.
At the end of his novels Daudet never descends
like a god from the machine to change character
in the twinkling of an eye, and to convert bad
men to good thoughts and good deeds.

He can give us goodness when he chooses, a
human goodness, not offensively perfect, not
priggish, not mawkish, but high-minded and
engaging. There are two such types in 'Kings
in Exile,' the Queen and Élysée Méraut, essentially honest both of them, thinking little of self,
and sustained by lofty purpose. Naturalistic
novelists generally (and M. Zola in particular)
live in a black world peopled mainly by fools and
knaves; from this blunder Daudet is saved by his
Southern temperament, by his lyric fervor, and,
at bottom, by his wisdom. He knows better; he
knows that while a weak creature like Christian II
is common, a resolute soul like Frédérique is
not so very rare. He knows that the contrast
and the clash of these characters is interesting
matter for the novelist. And no novelist has
had a happier inspiration than that which gave us
'Kings in Exile,' a splendid subject, splendidly
handled, and lending itself perfectly to the display of Daudet's best qualities, his poetry, his
ability to seize the actual, and his power of dealing with material such as the elder Dumas would
have delighted in with a restraint and a logic the

younger Dumas would have admired. Plot and
counter-plot, bravery, treachery, death — these
are elements for a Romanticist farrago; and in
Daudet's hands they are woven into a tapestry
almost as stiff as life itself. The stuff is Romantic enough, but the treatment is unhesitatingly
Realistic; and 'Kings in Exile,' better than any
other novel of Daudet's, explains his vogue with
readers of the most divergent tastes.

In the 'Nabob,' the romantic element is
slighter than in 'Kings in Exile'; the subject is
not so striking, and the movement of the story
is less straightforward. But what a panorama of
Paris it is that he unrolls before us in this story
of a luckless adventurer in the city of luxury then
under the control of the imperial band of brig-
ands! No doubt the Joyeuse family is an obtrusion and an artistic blemish, since they do not
logically belong in the scheme of the story; and
yet they (and their fellows in other books of
Daudet's) testify to his effort to get the truth
and the whole truth into his picture of Paris life.
Mora and Félicia Ruys and Jenkins, these are
the obverse of the medal, exposed in the shop-
windows that every passer-by can see. The Joyeuse girls and their father are the reverse, to be
viewed only by those who take the trouble to
look at the under side of things. They are sam-
ples of the simple, gentle, honest folk of whom

there must be countless thousands in France and even in its capital, but who fail to interest most French novelists just because they are not eccentric or wicked or ugly. Of a truth, Aline Joyeuse is as typically Parisian as Félicia Ruys herself; both are needed if the census is to be complete; and the omission of either is a source of error.

There is irony in Daudet's handling of these humbler figures, but it is compassionate and almost affectionate. If he laughs at Father Joyeuse there is no harshness and no hostility in his mirth. For the Joyeuse daughters he has indulgence and pity; and his humor plays about them and leaves them scart-free. It never stings them or scorches or sears, as it does Astier-Réhu and Christian II and the Prince of Axel, in spite of all his desire to be fair toward all the creatures of his brain.

Irony is only one of the manifestations of Daudet's humor. Wit he has also, and satire. And he is doubly fortunate in that he has both humor and the sense-of-humor — the positive and the negative. It is the sense-of-humor, so called, that many humorists are without, a deprivation which allows them to take themselves so seriously that they become a laughing-stock for the world. It is the sense-of-humor that makes the master of comedy, that helps him to see things in due proportion and perspective, that keeps him from exaggeration and emphasis, from sentimentality and melodrama and bathos. It is the sense-of-humor that prevents our making fools of ourselves; it is humor itself that softens our laughter at those who make themselves ridiculous. In his serious stories Daudet employs this negative humor chiefly, as though he had in memory La Bruyère's assertion that "he who makes us laugh is rarely able to win esteem for himself." His positive humor — gay, exuberant, contagious — finds its full field for display in some of the short-stories, and more especially in the Tartarin series.

Has any book of our time caused more laughter than 'Tartarin of Tarascon'—unless it be 'Tartarin on the Alps'? I can think only of one rival pair, 'Tom Sawyer' and 'Huckleberry Finn'—for Mark Twain and Alphonse Daudet both achieved the almost impossible feat of writing a successful sequel to a successful book, of forcing fortune to a repetition of a happy accident. The abundant laughter the French humorist excited is like that evoked by the American humorist—clean, hearty, healthy, self-respecting; it is in both cases what George Eliot in one of her letters called "the exquisite laughter that comes from a gratification of the reasoning faculty." Daudet and Mark Twain are imaginative Realists; their most amusing extravagance is but an exaggeration of the real thing; and they never let factitious fantasy sweep their feet off the ground. Tartarin is as typical of Provence as Colonel Sellers—to take that figure of Mark Twain's which is most like— is typical of the Mississippi valley.

Tartarin is as true as Numa Roumestan; in fact, they may almost be said to be sketched from the same model but in a very different temper. In 'Numa Roumestan' we are shown the sober side of the Southern temperament, the sorrow it brings in the house though it displays joy in the street; and in 'Tartarin' we behold only the immense comicality of the incessant incongruity between the word and the deed. Tartarin is Southern, it is true, and French; but he is very human also. There is a boaster and a liar in most of us, lying in wait for a chance to rush out and put us to shame. It is this universality of Daudet's satire that has given 'Tartarin' its vogue on both sides of the Atlantic. The ingenuity of Tartarin's misadventures, the variety of them in Algiers and in Switzerland, the obvious reason-ableness of them all, the delightful probability of these impossibilities, the frank gaiety and the unflagging high spirits — these are precious qualities, all of them; but it is rather the essen-tial humanness of Tartarin himself that has given him a reputation throughout the world. Very rarely indeed, now or in the past, has an author been lucky enough to add a single figure to the cosmopolitan gallery of fiction. Cervantes, Defoe, Swift, Le Sage, Dumas, have done it; Fielding and Hawthorne and Turgenieff have not.

It is no wonder that Daudet took pride in this. The real joy of the novelist, he declared, is to create human beings, to put on their feet types of humanity which thereafter circulate through the world with the name, the gesture, the grimace he has given them and which are cited and talked about without reference to their creator and without even any mention of him. And whenever Daudet heard some puppet of politics or literature called a Tartarin, a shiver ran through him —"the shiver of pride of a father, hidden in the crowd that is applauding his son and wanting all the time to cry out, 'That's my boy!'"

V

The time has not yet come for a final estimate of Daudet's position — if a time ever arrives when any estimate can be final. But already has a selection been made of the masterpieces which survive, and from which an author is judged by the next generation, that will have leisure to criticize only the most famous of the works this generation leaves behind it. We can see also that much of Daudet's later writing is slight and not up to his own high standard, although even his briefest trifle had always something of his charm, of his magic, of his seductive grace. We can see how rare an endowment he has when we note that he is an acute observer of mankind, and yet without any taint of misanthropy, and that he combines fidelity of reproduction with poetic elevation.

He is — to say once more what has already been said in these pages more than once — he is a lover of romance with an unfaltering respect for reality. We all meet with strange experiences once in our lives, with "things you could put in a story," as the phrase is; but we none of us have hairbreadth escapes every morning before breakfast. The romantic is as natural as anything else; it is the excess of the romantic which is in bad taste. It is the piling up of the agony which is disgusting. It is the accumulation upon one impossible hero of many exceptional adventures which is untrue and therefore immoral. Daudet's most individual peculiarity was his skill in seizing the romantic aspects of the commonplace. In one of his talks with his son he said that a novelist must beware of an excess of lyric enthusiasm; he himself sought for emotion, and emotion escaped when human proportions were exceeded. Balance, order, reserve, symmetry, sobriety — these are the qualities he was ever praising. The real, the truthful, the sincere — these are what he sought always to attain.

Daudet may lack the poignant intensity of Balzac, the lyric sweep of Hugo, the immense architectural strength of M. Zola, the implacable disinterestedness of Flaubert, the marvelous concentration of Maupassant, but he has more humor than any of them and more charm — more sympathy than any but Hugo, and more sincerity than any but Flaubert. His is perhaps a rarer combination than any of theirs — the gift of story-telling, the power of character-drawing, the grasp of emotional situation, the faculty of analysis, the feeling for form, the sense of style, an unfailing and humane interest in his fellow-men, and an irresistible desire to tell the truth about life as he saw it with his own eyes.

(1898)

VI

ON A NOVEL OF THACKERAY'S

[This essay was written as one of a series in 'My Favorite Novelist and his Best Book,' appearing in *Munsey's Magazine*.]

ON A NOVEL OF THACKERAY'S

AS the author of 'Uncle Tom's Cabin' once wrote to the author of 'Silas Marner,' "So many stories are tramping over one's mind in every modern magazine, nowadays, that one is macadamized, so to speak"; and therefore it is good for one to be forced, now and again, to plow up one's mind, as it were, that the seed falling by the wayside may have a chance to take root. To let light and air into the mind, to admit the refreshing water that stimulates to renewed activity, nothing is fitter than the cultivation of the habit of comparative criticism. For those of us who love books and reading—if I may now leave the fields for the library—it is well always to set the newer claimants for fame beside the old masters, to measure them without prejudice, and to weigh them in the equal scales. And so I should welcome the call to choose out of all the host of story-tellers the craftsman whose work most delights me, and to deliver the reasons for the faith that is in me—were it not for one insuperable obstacle to any such selection.

This difficulty is easy to define: it is simply that no true lover of books and reading can be expected to limit his liking to the works of any one author. He is not so poor as to have only one favorite; he resembles rather the Sultan in having a harem full of them. Mr. Howells reminded us, not long ago, that man is still imperfectly monogamous; and whatever may be thought of this assertion when applied to life, it is absolutely true when applied to literature. He who marries a single book is likely, sooner or later, to weary of its charms and to seek a divorce, that he may bestow his affection upon another subject. Though he be no universal lover, the bookman is often mutable and swiftly inconstant.

No man who can read and write and taste what he reads is so narrow-minded as to confine himself solely to the writings of a single author. His moods must vary with the revolving seasons and with the lapse of years. In the spring the Greek lyrists may charm him who in midwinter delighted rather in the Elizabethan dramatists. The romance of adventure stirs his blood in youth; later in life, when he knows the world better, he finds his account rather in the novel of character, with its flashes of self-revelation. For

myself, I have outworn my relish for Poe's tales,
gruesome or melancholic, although I esteem his
art not lower than I did; and the artifice of Sheridan's comedies palls upon me now, although
once I held them to be the perfection of wit.

To-day the list is long of novelists in whose
books I can lose myself with satisfaction; the
list is long and of a most cosmopolitan com-
plexion. As I visualize it in a column, I find
American and British names, French and Russian.
There is Thackeray, for one, and for another,
Thackeray's master, Balzac. There is Hawthorne, and there is Turgenieff, Hawthorne's
rival in ethical richness and in constructive symmetry. There is Mr. Howells, with his incarnation of the more sophisticated American as he is
seen to-day on the Atlantic seaboard; and there
is Mark Twain, with his resuscitation of the more
primitive American as he was to be discerned
once upon a time on the banks of the Mississippi.

All these pleasure me at one time or another.
I cannot tell how often I have read the 'Scarlet
Letter' and 'Smoke,' 'Henry Esmond' and 'Père
Goriot,' the 'Rise of Silas Lapham' and the 'Adventures of Huckleberry Finn.' To make a choice
of them is frankly impossible, or even to say that
these six are the favorite half-dozen. But if a
selection is imperative, I am ready, for the moment at least, to declare that Thackeray is the

novelist I would rather discuss here and now, well aware that no favorite has a right to expect a long continuance in grace. And the reason why I pick out Thackeray from among the other novelists I like as well as I like him (if not better) is that I may thus call attention to a book of his which I believe to be somewhat neglected. I hold this book to be his best artistically, the one most to be respected, if not the one to be regarded with the most warmth. It is perhaps the only story of Thackeray's which the majority of his readers have never taken up. It is the tale of his telling which most clearly reveals some of his best qualities and which most artfully masks some of his worst defects. It is the ' Memoirs of Barry Lyndon, Esq., Written by Himself.'

It was published originally in a British magazine, and so little liked at first that it was not republished as a book for many years—indeed, not until after ' Vanity Fair ' and ' Henry Esmond ' had at last revealed Thackeray's genius, and lent interest even to the timid firstlings of his muse. " If the secret history of books could be written," so he told us in the pages of ' Pendennis,' " and the author's private thoughts and meanings noted down alongside of his story, how many insipid volumes would become interesting and dull tales excite the reader." ' Barry Lyndon ' is neither insipid nor dull; yet its secret history would be interesting enough. It was written when Thackeray was not yet thirty-five years of age—for he flowered late, like most of the greater novelists. Born in 1811, he was married in 1836; and in 1840 he had been forced to place his wife in confinement. Two years later he made a tour in Ireland, the record of which we can read in the 'Irish Sketch-Book,' published in 1843; and in 1844 he followed these Hibernian sketches with the full-length portrait of the Irish Barry. It was not until 1847 that 'Vanity Fair' began to appear; and the veracious history of Colonel Henry Esmond was not given to the world until 1852.

After these later stories beamed forth, the earlier tale shone with a reflected light only; and yet I cannot but think it to be Thackeray's highest achievement as an artist in letters. Perhaps, if 'Barry Lyndon' had not unfortunately failed of appreciation, Thackeray might have taken his art more seriously in the broader and deeper fictions he set before us afterward. In them the prevailing faults are an affectation of knowingness, an excess of sentiment, an obtruded moralizing, a tendency toward caricature (due, probably, to the overwhelming vogue of Dickens), a looseness of structure (due, perhaps, to the mode of publication in monthly parts), a confidential manner, and a personal intervention of the showman constantly reminding us that the puppets are but the work of his hands after all.

In 'Barry Lyndon' the defects are minimized or disappear altogether. The knowingness which is almost offensive when Arthur Pendennis is telling us about the Newcomes is a touch of character when it is Barry Lyndon who sets forth his own adventures, appealing to the reader as a man of the world, or else the hero will not be viewed from the proper perspective. The fact that Barry himself is the narrator prevents any overplus of moralizing or sentiment. The confidential manner is proper enough in an autobiography, which has the further advantage of forbidding the appearance of the showman in front of the figure he is manipulating. The fact that the book deals with but the chosen episodes of one man's career gives it a unity not found in any other of Thackeray's works except 'Henry Esmond'; and, except 'Esmond,' again, no story of Thackeray's is so free from caricature as 'Barry Lyndon.'

Those of us who prefer the impersonal and impassive method of story-telling used by Mérimée and Flaubert, by Hawthorne and Turgenieff, in which the author seems never to intervene, but only to set down the inevitable actions of his characters, are annoyed by the malignity with which Thackeray pursues Becky Sharp; we feel that he is guilty of meanness in taking sides against one of his own creations. We are disturbed by the reflections with which he pads the chapters of his novels,—although we hold that his vagabond moralizing is delightful in the 'Roundabout Papers,' since it is the privilege of the essayist to be discursive. Thackeray has a native bias toward the didactic, but no doubt he felt he had the warrant of Fielding, and claimed the right to revive the intercalary essays of 'Tom Jones.' Yet in Fielding's case these invocations of the muse, these discussions of the art of prose epic, these comments on character, were frankly prefixed to the several books of 'Tom Jones'; they were, as who should say, a series of prefaces to successive volumes, while Thackeray's digressions exist for their own sake, and arrive, seemingly, whenever the fabulist is out of matter.

Twice only was Thackeray able to conquer this bias—in 'Henry Esmond' and in 'Barry Lyndon.' These are his only novels in the form of autobiography, whence we may infer that this imposed on him a needed reserve. Of the various ways in which fiction may be presented to the reader—the novel in letters and the novel in dialogue, the novel told in the third person and the novel told in the first person—the last is the best for self-revelation and for adventure. Is not the interest of 'Robinson Crusoe' doubled for us by our knowledge that it is the castaway himself who is recording his shipwrecks and his prayers?

Perhaps 'Barry Lyndon' is not so flawless in structure nor so substantially planned as 'Henry Esmond.' In general, Thackeray gave little heed to the architectonics of fiction; he was an improviser, as Scott was; and the evolution of most of his novels is fortuitous, even though he never repeated the blunder of the bifurcated plot which is the chiefest blemish of 'Vanity Fair'—as it is also of 'Anna Karénina.' It may be that the autobiographic form forced Thackeray to the forethought he more than often shirked; so it happens that these two stories have each its own unity, and are not mere congeries of straggling episodes.

But if the framework of 'Barry Lyndon' is a little less artfully proportioned than that of 'Henry Esmond,' this is its only inferiority. In sustaining the assumed tone the earlier book is far superior to the later, and the task was far more dangerous. Thackeray had made 'Esmond' in his own image; well aware of his own tendency to preach, he endowed the colonel with a ready willingness to point a moral, in season and out; and he confessed to Trollope that the impeccable hero was a bit of a prig. Henry Esmond is a perfect gentleman at all times, and Barry Lyndon is ever an unblushing rascal; and while the portrayal of the former was not difficult to Thackeray, there is greater gusto, I think, in the picture of the latter, and a more consummate art.

In the one we find the life of a good man, whose sweetness and light are almost cloying at times; and in the other we follow the career of a bad man, whose unblushing knavery is spread before us with unfailing irony. As Thackeray paints the portrait, it is worthy to hang in any rogues' gallery—as the original was worthy to be hanged on any scaffold. The villain double-dyed is very rare in modern fiction, and Barry Lyndon is an altogether incomparable scoundrel, who believes in himself, tells us his own misdeeds, and ever proclaims himself a very fine fellow—and honestly expects us to take him at his own valuation, while all our knowledge of his evil doings is derived from his own self-laudatory statements! This device of transparency Thackeray derived direct from Miss Edgeworth, I think—with perhaps some memory of Fielding's use of it. The tale of 'Castle Rackrent' is also put in the mouth of one who is forever praising those whom we despise at once, although all our information about them comes to us from the self-appointed eulogist. "It takes two to speak the truth," said Thoreau; "one to speak, and another to hear."

Certain depths of the Irish character Miss Edgeworth sounded in that story—its wit, its humor, its loyalty, its clannishness, its irresponsibility;

and, of course, Thackeray profited by the work
of his predecessor. His book was perhaps a reaction from the more rollicking romances of Lover
and Lever, at the height of their popularity when
'Barry Lyndon' was published; and it was like
them in its prevailing tone of sadness. About
this time Thackeray wrote the essay on a 'Box of
Novels,' and declared that "from 'Castle Rackrent' downward, every Hibernian tale that I have
read is sure to leave a sort of woful tender impression." It may be that this melancholy it is
that has kept many a reader away from both
'Barry Lyndon' and 'Castle Rackrent.' It may
be, also, that most of those who turn to fiction
for an amusement insist upon a straightforward
story that a man may read as he runs; and they
resent the needless trouble imposed upon them
by the use of irony.

Sometimes I venture to think that Miss Edgeworth has more confidence in the device of transparency than Thackeray has, or else she puts
more trust in the intelligence of her readers.
While Thady is unfailingly unconscious of the
effect of his revelations upon those he is addressing, the mask of Barry is lowered now and again,
and Thackeray speaks out of his own mouth.
It is the author who sentimentalizes over the
widow of Roaring Harry Barry of Barryville,
and not her own son Redmond; and yet per-

haps the thought might be the son's after all, and only the overstatement of it the author's. The reflections upon the horrors of war at the end of the fourth chapter are Thackeray's own; or at least they were made by Colonel Henry Esmond, and not by Corporal Redmond Barry; they have merely wandered into the wrong autobiography. Madame de Lilliengarten's narrative of the downfall of the princess is rather Thackeray's account than her own; what she saw, she saw through Thackeray's large spectacles; or her views and the author's seem to be presented to us simultaneously, to combine as in the stereoscope. Once (in Chapter XVII it is) the author even sinks to step into the story and in a foot-note to explain that Barry is no mere hero of romance, but a callous brute; and this inartistic comment appears doubly needless when we read a few pages further and find the husband protesting in self-defense that "for the first three years I never struck my wife but when I was in liquor," and asseverating that when he flung the carving-knife at her son, he was drunk, "as everybody present can testify." An author who can make a character strip his soul by strokes like these must heartily despise his audience if he feels called upon to come before the curtain, pointer in hand, and expound the real meaning of his drama.

Barry has a conceit so sublime that it allows

him to set down the most disparaging remarks against himself with a magnificent assurance that nobody could possibly believe any such accusation against him. When his uncle and confederate praises his "indomitable courage, swagger, and audacity," he denies the swagger "*in toto*, being always most modest in my demeanor." He is perpetually boasting about this modesty of his. There was never such a braggart; and he had his fine qualities, too. When in funds he was openhanded, as gamblers and spendthrifts are wont to be. When it suited his purpose or his whim, he was kindly; but when his own evil ends demanded it, he was adamant. He respects the spirit of those who withstood him stanchly, and he had no scruple as to the means whereby he sought to overcome them. He is the boldest and most resolute devil in all the novels of the nineteenth century—with the possible exception of Vautrin; and to find his equal we must pass from fiction to fact and compare him with that typical adventurer of the eighteenth century, Jacques Casanova de Seingalt.

If the method of Thackeray's book is Miss Edgeworth's, the model for its hero is Casanova. The stout heart of the Irishman and his ignoble soul are the Italian's also. In Chapter XIII the theory of winning women by attacking them was learned by the private of Bülow's regiment from the prisoner of Venice; and in the same chapter the list of the women Barry made love to is only a faint echo of the Leporello roll of that moral leper, Seingalt. The strain on the convention of all fictitious autobiography—that the turns of a conversation can be recalled at will after many years—is no greater in the recollections of Barry Lyndon than in the octogenarian reminiscences of Casanova. It is indisputable that Thackeray was familiar enough with this startling record of the unspeakable moral squalor of continental Europe in the years before the French Revolution; the name of Casanova appears once in the pages of this book, and that of Seingalt a second time; and a friend of mine once owned Thackeray's copy of Casanova's autobiography with the novelist's signature on the title.

Barry Lyndon, splendid scoundrel as he presents himself, is not the only broadly limned character in the book. Quite as fine is the stern veracity of the portrayal of Lady Lyndon, unspoiled by any touch of sentimentality. Her son, Bullington, is as boldly drawn; and so is the one-eyed chevalier (d'industrie), Barry's uncle. And the story itself has an unflagging interest and a dramatic picturesqueness not frequent in Thackeray's easy-going fictions. Perhaps no single scene is as subtly penetrative as Becky Sharp's admiration of her husband when he thrashes Lord Steyne, or as finely romantic as Henry Esmond's breaking of his sword before the prince. But nowhere else has Thackeray raised himself to so high a pitch of tragic terror as in the account of the death of the devoted princess struggling vainly against her inevitable, inexorable doom.

With all these manifold merits, why is 'Barry Lyndon' neglected? It is ignored not merely by the broad public, which perhaps resents having a villain palmed on it for a hero, but also by Thackeray's friendliest critics. Trollope praises it briefly, but with inadequate appreciation. Mr. Andrew Lang casually calls it a masterpiece, and says no more. Mr. Frederic Harrison says nothing at all. And Bagehot had said nothing, either; but one remark of Bagehot's may partly explain the matrimonial career of both Henry Esmond and Barry Lyndon: "Women much respect real virtue; they much admire strong and successful immorality."

(1897)

VII

H. C. BUNNER

H. C. BUNNER [1]

O NLY a few weeks ago death put an end to
a friendship that had endured for nine-
teen years—nearly the half of my friend's life, as
it happened, for he was but forty when he died,
and only a little less than the half of mine; and
in all these years of our manhood there had never
been the shadow of a cloud over the friendship.
We had lived in the same house for a while; we
had collaborated more than once; we had talked
over our plans together; we had criticized each
other's writings; we had revised each other's
proof-sheets; and there was between us never
any misunderstanding or doubt, nor any word of
disagreement. I never went to Bunner for counsel or for aid that I did not get it, freely and sympathetically given, and always exactly what I
needed. Sympathy was, indeed, the key-note of
Bunner's character, and cheery helpfulness was
chief of his characteristics. To me the com-

[1] Born at Oswego, New York, August 3, 1855; died at Nutley, New Jersey, May 11, 1896.

panionship was of inestimable benefit; and it is bitter to face a future when I can no more hope for his hearty greeting, for the welcoming glance of his eager eye, for the solid grip of his hand, and for the unfailing stimulus and solace of his conversation.

It was late in the winter of 1877 that I made Bunner's acquaintance, three or four weeks after the first number of *Puck* had been issued in English. In the fall of 1876 Messrs. Keppler & Schwarzmann had started a German comic paper with colored cartoons, and it had been so well received that they were persuaded to accept Mr. Sydney Rosenfeld's suggestion to get out an edition in the English language also, utilizing the same cuts and caricatures. Bunner had already aided Mr. Rosenfeld in a journalistic venture which had died young; and he was the first man asked to join the small staff of the new weekly.

He was then barely twenty-two years old, but he had already had not a little experience in journalism. Educated at Dr. Callisen's school, he had been prepared for Columbia College; but at the last minute he had given up his college career, much as Washington Irving had chosen to do three quarters of a century earlier. When he took his place as a clerk in an importing house— an experience that was to give him an invaluable knowledge of the ways of mercantile New York

—he had supplemented his schooling by much browsing along the shelves of the library of his maternal uncle, Henry T. Tuckerman. He had taken Thoreau's advice to "read the best books first, or you may not have a chance to read them at all." When he gave up this place and trusted to his pen to make a living he had his British essayists at the ends of his fingers and his British poets at the tip of his tongue. He had been brought up on Shakspere. He was a fair Latinist, and it is rare to find a lover of Horace whose own style lacks savor. While he was writing for the *Arcadian*, another short-lived journal, he had been able to increase his acquaintance with the latter-day literatures of France and Germany. This was an equipment far richer than that of the ordinary young man who becomes an assistant on a comic paper.

The early numbers of *Puck* abound in evidences of Bunner's manifold qualifications for his new position. He had wide reading to give flavor to his writing; he had wit, he had humor, he was a master of parody in prose and verse, he had invention and ingenuity and unfailing freshness, and above all he had the splendid fecundity of confident youth. The staff of the paper was very small, and little money could be spent for outside contributions; and there were many weeks when nearly half of the whole number was written by Bunner. More than half of the good things in *Puck* were Bunner's, as I discovered when I paid my first visit to the office.

I had contributed to Mr. Rosenfeld's earlier venture, and when the new journal was started I opened communication with him again. One day I was asked to call. The office of *Puck* was then in a dingy building in North William Street, since torn down to make room for the Brooklyn Bridge. Mr. Rosenfeld met me at the street door, and after our first greetings we passed by the printing machinery on the ground floor and began our ascent to the editorial room in an upper story. I complimented Mr. Rosenfeld on something in the current number of *Puck*—I forget now what it was, but I think it was a certain 'Ballad of Burdens.' "Bunner wrote that," I was informed by Mr. Rosenfeld, who had a hearty appreciation of his fellow-worker's ability. As we toiled up the next flight of stairs I praised something else I had seen in the pages of *Puck*, and Mr. Rosenfeld responded, "That was Bunner's too." On the third landing I commended yet another contribution, only to be told for the third time that Bunner was the author of this also. Then we entered the bare loft, at one end of which the artists had their drawing-tables, while at the other end stood the sole editorial desk. And there I had the pleasure of shaking hands with the writer of the various articles I had admired. He was beardless and slim, and, in spite of his glasses, he impressed me as being very young indeed. He had ardor, vivacity, and self-possession, and it did not take me long to discover that his comrades held him in high esteem. As for myself, I liked him at first glance; and that afternoon a friendship was founded which endured as long as his life.

A few weeks later Mr. Rosenfeld and Messrs. Keppler & Schwarzmann disagreed and he left the paper. Then Bunner succeeded to the editorship. In those days *Puck* was still but an experiment, and it was long doubtful whether or not it would survive, since none of its countless predecessors had been able to do so. That it did not die young, as *Vanity Fair* had died and *Mrs. Grundy* and *Punchinello*, was due, I think, to the fortunate combination of the caricaturing adroitness of Joseph Keppler, the business sense of Mr. Schwarzmann, and the editorial resourcefulness of Bunner. To apportion the credit exactly among these three is impossible and unnecessary: the qualities of all three were really indispensable to the ultimate strength of the new weekly. It was not long after Bunner became editor that the circulation of the edition of *Puck* printed in English began to gain on the circulation of the edition printed in German; and after a while the owners discovered that instead of having a German paper with an offshoot in English they had in fact a paper in English with an annex in German. Bunner it was who acted as a medium between the German originators of *Puck* and the American public. No paper could have had a more loyal editor, and for years Bunner put the best of his strength into its pages. He had been known to say that, after his family, his first thought was for *Puck*.

At first he did not care for politics, taking more interest in literature, in the drama, and in art, and having given little thought to public affairs. But he soon saw how great an influence might be wielded by the editor of a comic paper who should accompany the political cartoon with persuasive comment; and with this perception came a sense of his own responsibility. He began at once to reason out for himself the principles which should govern political action. He did his own thinking in politics as in literature; he was as independent as he was patriotic. In Lowell's essay on Lincoln we are told that even at the outbreak of the Rebellion there were not wanting among us men " who had so steeped their brains in London literature as to mistake cockneyism for European culture, and contempt of their country for cosmopolitan breadth of view." To say that Bunner was wholly free from any taint of Anglomania is to state the case mildly; his Ameri-

canism was as sturdy as Lowell's. He was firmly
rooted in the soil of his nativity. He was glad
that he was an American and proud of being a
New-Yorker. He saw that creatures of the type
that Lowell scorned still lingered on; and if he
was intolerant toward any one it was toward
the renegade American—the man without a
country.

But Bunner was rarely intolerant. His imagination was quick enough to let him understand
why those who opposed him should hold a different view of the duty of the moment, and he
set himself to the task of persuading his oppo-
nents. He met them, not with invective, but
with an appeal to their reason. And this is the
way in which he was able to make the editorial
page of *Puck* a power for good in the land. In
its nature journalism must be ephemeral; and
perhaps it was to be expected that the work
Bunner did in inciting his readers to independence
of thought is already half forgotten, and that it
never even received the full recognition it deserved.

Until the nomination of Mr. Blaine in 1884 *Puck*
might have been called an independent Republi-
can paper; but after the nomination of Mr. Cleveland *Puck* was an independent Democratic paper.
Bunner greatly admired the stalwart manliness of
Mr. Cleveland's character. He was like the Presi-

dent in that he had made no special study of economics until a consideration of the tariff was forced upon him. This seemed to him a question to be solved by common sense; and having found a solution satisfactory to his own mind, he thought he could bring others over to his way of thinking, if he reasoned with them calmly, assuming that they knew no more than he did and that they were as disinterested as he and as intelligent. Perhaps it was even an advantage to him then that he had taken to the study of this problem only a little while before, for he had thus a closer understanding of the frame of mind in which the voters were whom he wished to convince. Certainly nothing less academic can well be imagined than Bunner's discussion of the tariff. He was dignified always, and direct, and plain-spoken; and above all he was persuasive—a great novelty in the dispute between protection and free trade. Bunner held that hard words, even if they broke no bones, changed no man's opinions; and what he sought was not an occasion for self-display but a chance to make converts. He met the men he addressed on their own level and with neither condescension nor affectation of superiority; and his manner invited them to talk the matter over quietly. In argument he acted on Tocqueville's maxim that " he who despises mankind will never get the best out of either

others or himself." He explained that there was
no cause for any excitement and that the subject
was really far simpler than most people thought;
and having thus won willing listeners, he set
forth his own views, very clearly and with every-
day illustrations.

Bunner was at first not only the editor of the
journal, responsible for all that went into it, for
the letterpress and for the cuts and for the mechanical make-up: he was also the chief contributor, as he had been when Mr. Rosenfeld was
in charge. What a comic paper needs above all
is not a group of brilliant wits sending in their
best things whenever the inspiration chances to
strike them: it is the steady and trustworthy
writers who can be counted on regularly, week
in and week out, to supply "comic copy" not
below a certain average. Bunner was very much
more than a mere manufacturer of "comic copy,"
but he could act in this capacity also when need
was.

Into the broad columns of *Puck* during the first
ten years of its existence Bunner poured an end-
less stream of humorous matter in prose and in
verse. Whatever might be wanted he stood
ready to supply—rimes of the times, humorous
ballads, *vers de société*, verses to go with a cartoon, dialogues to go under a drawing, paragraphs pertinent and impertinent, satiric sketches

of character, short-stories, little comedies, non-descript comicalities of all kinds. Whatever the demand upon him, he was ready and able to meet it; he had irresistible freshness and dauntless fecundity. No doubt very much of this comic journalism was no better than it pretended to be; but, on the other hand, the average was surprisingly high and the variety was extraordinary. And it is to be noted that in even the slightest specimen of Bunner's "comic copy" it was impossible not to see that the writer was a gentleman, that his was not a bitter wit, and that he had always the gentle kindliness of the true humorist.

For one figure especially that Bunner evoked in those days of struggle I had always a keen liking. That was the character of V. Hugo Dusenberry, the professional poet, prepared to ply for hire, to fill all orders promptly, to give you verse while you wait, and to write poems in every style, satisfaction guaranteed. This was a delightful conception, with a tinge of burlesque in it, no doubt, and perhaps without the restraint of Bunner's more mature art. V. Hugo Dusenberry enlivened the pages of many a number of *Puck*; and more than once in later years I urged on Bunner the advisability of making a selection of the professional poet's verses and of his lectures on the art; but Bunner's finer taste deemed this sketch too broad in its effects, too temporary in its allusions—in a word, too journalistic—for revival between the covers of a book. Yet he had reveled in the writing of the V. Hugo Dusenberry papers, and they gave him scope to develop his marvelous gift of parody.

It has always seemed to me that Bunner was one of the great parodists of the nineteenth century. Not Smith's 'Rejected Addresses,' not Thackeray's 'Prize Novelists,' not Mr. Bret Harte's 'Condensed Novels,' not Bayard Taylor's 'Diversions of the Echo Club,' shows a sharper understanding of the essentials of another author's art or a swifter faculty for reproducing them, than Bunner revealed in these V. Hugo Dusenberry papers, or in his 'Home, Sweet Home, with Variations' (now included in his 'Airs from Arcady'). There are two kinds of parody, as we all know. One is a mere imitation of the external form and is commonly inexpensive and tiresome. The other is rarer and calls for an evocation of the internal spirit; and it was in the accomplishment of this that Bunner excelled. His parodies were never unfair and never unkind; they were not degraded reproductions of what another author had done, but rather imaginative suggestions as to what he might do had he chosen to treat these subjects in this way. In other words, Bunner met the author he desired to imitate on that author's own ground and tried a fall with him there.   I doubt if any passage of Walt Whitman's own verse is more characteristically pathetic than the one in Bunner's 'Home, Sweet Home, with Variations,' in which the return of the convict son is set before us with a few tense strokes. In prose he was equally felicitous, as all will admit who recall the reproduction of Sterne ('A Sentimental Annex') and who remember the imitations of Mr. Frank R. Stockton and of Mr. Rudyard Kipling, in which he managed to put himself somehow into the skins of these diverse authors and to spin for us yarns of theirs of which they themselves need not have been ashamed. Readers of 'Rowen' may be reminded of the airy little lyric called 'Imitation,' which begins:

> My love she leans from the window
> Afar in a rosy land;
> And red as a rose are her blushes,
> And white as a rose her hand; :

and which ends:

> This German style of poem
> Is uncommonly popular now;
> For the worst of us poets can do it—
> Since Heine showed us how.

And yet this chameleon gift did not interfere at all with Bunner's own originality. Just as the painter studies his trade in the studio of a master, so the man of letters (whether he knows it or not) is bound prentice to one or more of his elders in the art, from whom he learns the secrets of the craft. The acute analysis Bunner had made of the methods of other writers aided him to recognize those most suitable for his own use, and thus his individuality was like the melancholy of Jaques, "compounded of many simples." None the less was it Bunner's own, and quite unmistakable. In verse he was in his youth a pupil of Heine's, and for a season he studied under Mr. Austin Dobson; but he would be a dull reader of ' Airs from Arcady' who did not discover that in whatever workshops Bunner had spent his wander-years, he had come home with a style of his own.

So in fiction he was a close student of Boccaccio, that consummate artist in narrative. He delighted in the swiftness and in the symmetry of the best tales in the ' Decameron,' in their deftness of construction, in their omission of all trivial details, in their sharpness of outline. I have heard him say that when he was turning over in his mind the plot of a new story and found himself in doubt as to the best way of handling it, he was wont to take up the ' Decameron,' not merely for mental refreshment, but because he was certain to find in it the solution of the problem that puzzled him, and to discover somewhere in Boccaccio's pages a model for the tale he was trying to tell. And yet how wide apart are the Italian's somber or merry narratives and the American's sunny and hopeful 'Love in Old Cloathes' and 'As One Having Authority' and 'Zadoc Pine.'

When the late Guy de Maupassant (who was like Boccaccio in more ways than one) suddenly revealed his marvelous mastery of the art of story-telling, Bunner became his disciple for a while, and even thought to apply the Frenchman's methods to American subjects, the result being the very amusing volume called 'Short Sixes.' But so thoroughly had Bunner transmuted Maupassant's formulas that he would need to be a preternaturally keen-eyed critic who could detect in this volume any sign of the American's indebtedness to his French contemporary. Perhaps a little to Bunner's surprise, no one of his books is more characteristically his own than 'Short Sixes'; and perhaps this was the motive that led him afterward to produce 'Made in France,' in which he undertook lovingly to Americanize some half-score of Maupassant's stories, declaring in his preface that although the venture may seem somewhat bold, it was undertaken in a spirit of sincerest and faithfulest admiration for him who "must always be, to my thinking, the best of story-tellers since Boccaccio wrote down the tales he heard from women's lips." In a spirit of tricksy humor that Maupassant would have appreciated, the most French of all these ten tales "with a United States twist" is not derived from the French but is Bunner's own invention—a fact no reviewer of the volume ever knew enough to find out.

Like Boccaccio, and like Maupassant, Bunner succeeded best in the short-story, the *novella*, the *conte*. His longer fictions are not full-fledged novels; they are rather short-stories writ large. From this criticism must be excepted the first of them, an early novel, 'A Woman of Honor,' which was founded on an unacted play of his. He came in time to dislike the 'Woman of Honor' as artificial, not to say theatrical; and it must be admitted that this youthful story lacks the firmer qualities of his later works; yet it proved that he had power to invent incident and strength to construct a plot.

There was nothing theatrical and scarcely anything that was artificial in either of the novels that followed, in the 'Midge' or in the 'Story of a New York House,' beautiful tales both of them, quite as ingenious as the earlier story, but far simpler in movement and far finer in the delicacy of character-drawing. Perhaps the salient characteristics of these two brief novels are the unforced pathos the author could command at will, his sympathy with the loser in the wager of life, and his sentiment, which never sickened into sentimentality. Perhaps their chief merit, in the eyes of many, was that they were novels of New York, the result of a long and loving study of this great town of ours.

It was one of Bunner's prejudices—and he was far too human to be without many of them— that New York is one of the most interesting places in the world. He enjoyed its powerful movement, its magnificent vitality. He took pleasure in observing the manners and customs of its kaleidoscopic population. He thrilled with the sense of its might to-day, and he gloried in its historic past. For himself he took pride also in that he came of an old New York stock. As he wrote in 'Rowen':

> Why do I love New York, my dear?
> I do not know. Were my father here—
> And *his*—and HIS—the three and I
> Might, perhaps, make you some reply.

Bunner had discovered for himself the truth of Lowell's assertion that "however needful it may be to go abroad for the study of esthetics, a man may find here also pretty bits of what may be called the social picturesque, and little landscapes over which the Indian-summer atmosphere of the

past broods as sweetly and tenderly as over a
Roman ruin." Noisy and restless as New York
is, and blatant as it may seem to some, those
who have eyes and a willingness to see can collect specimens not only of the social picturesque,
but of the physical picturesque also. Into the
'Midge' and into the 'Story of a New York
House' Bunner put the results of his investigations into the life about us in the great city, to the
most interesting manifestations of which so many
of us are hopelessly blind. In the 'Midge' he
sketched what was then the French quarter, lying
south of Washington Square; and in the 'Story
of a New York House' he showed how a home
once far outside of the town was in time swal-
lowed up as the streets advanced, and how at
last it was left neglected as the district sank into
disrepute; and the story of the edifice wherein
the family dwelt that built it is the tragic story
also of the family itself.

Not a few of Bunner's twoscore short-stories
were also studies of human nature as it has been
developed nowadays in the Manhattan environment. And not a few of them were studies of
human nature as it has been developed in the
semi-rural region that lies within the radius of an
hour's journey from New York. In this territory
are the homes of thousands whose work takes
them daily to the city, while they spend their

nights in the country. Bunner had an extended acquaintance with the manners and customs of the hybrid being created by the immense expansion of the metropolis; and this was in fact only self-knowledge after all, since seven or eight years before his death he had gone to dwell in the pretty village of Nutley, which he came to love dearly—and in which at last he was to die. His sense-of-humor was singularly acute, and he was swift to perceive the many shades of difference by which the suburban residents are set off from country people on the one hand and on the other from city folks. But his sympathy was broad here as elsewhere, and his observation of character was never harsh or hostile, whether it was the urban type he had in hand, or the suburban and semi-rural, or the truly rural.

Perhaps the ripest of his books is 'Jersey Street and Jersey Lane; Urban and Suburban Sketches.' The tales and essays in this volume have not the brisk fun and the hearty comicality of 'Short Sixes,' but they are mellow with a more mature perception of the truth that, as Sam Slick says, "there is a great deal of nature in human nature." He had the sharp insight of a humorist, it is true, and the swift appreciation of the unexpected oddities of character; but he had in abundance also the gentle delicacy of the poet— not that even those urban and suburban sketches are nerveless in the least, or sappy. 'The Lost Child' is as vigorous in its way as even 'Zadoc Pine.' It is rather that the essential manliness of Bunner's writing is here accompanied by an almost feminine delicacy of feeling. And yet to praise 'Jersey Street and Jersey Lane' for possessing this quality is perhaps to suggest unfairly that his other prose was without it. What I wished to convey is rather that in this last book of his the strength and the sweetness are even more harmoniously combined than in any of the earlier volumes. He had come to a mastery of his tools, and his hand worked without faltering. Even at the outset of his career as a man of letters, Bunner was not a story-teller merely by the grace of God—as is many a novelist who now and again may hold the ear of the public for a little while. He was always a devoted student of the art and mystery of narrative. He was born with the gift of story-telling, it is true; but it was by thought and by toil and by unending care that he made of himself the accomplished craftsman in fiction that he became before he died.

Although 'Zadoc Pine,' with its stalwart Americanism and its needed lesson of independence, has always been a chief favorite of my own, probably the first series of 'Short Sixes' has been the most popular of all Bunner's volumes of fiction. And it is very likely that here again

the broad public is right in its preference.   I can
see how it is that 'Short Sixes' may strike many
as the most characteristic of Bunner's collections
of tales.   In this book he is perhaps more frankly
a humorist than in any other; and Bunner's humor
was not biting, not saturnine, not boisterous; it
was not contorted nor extravagant nor violent;
it flowed freely and spontaneously.   Above all, it
was friendly; it blossomed out of our common
human nature.

I do not think that the wide-spread liking for
these 'Short Sixes' was due chiefly to their vivacity, to their spontaneity, to their cleverness,
to their originality, to their unfailing fertility of
invention, to their individuality—although of
course all these qualities were recognized and
each helped in due proportion.   I think they were
taken to heart by the broad public because in
them the author revealed himself most completely; because in them he showed clearly the
simplicity of his own character—its transparency,
so to speak; because in them could be seen
abundantly his own kindliness, gentleness, toleration—in a word, his own broad sympathy even
with the absurd persons he might be laughing at.
Being a gentleman and a scholar, Bunner understood the ways of a man of the world and could
record the sayings and doings of a woman of
fashion; but being a man also and a good Ameri-

can, he had a liking for the plain people as well, and an understanding of their habits of living and of their modes of thought. It was his fellow-man who interested Bunner above all else; and this feeling his fellow-man reciprocated.

Perhaps the chief charm of Bunner's verses is also a result of this same sympathy. As Hazlitt tells us, "Poetry is the universal language which the heart holds with nature and itself." Often *vers de société* (the English translation "society verse" is painfully inadequate)—often *vers de société* which may meet the triple test of being brief and brilliant and buoyant is also hard and narrow and cynical. Some of Prior's best pieces are cold, and some of Praed's are chilly, to say the least. A more human warmth flushes the equally delightful stanzas of the late Frederick Locker-Lampson and of Mr. Austin Dobson. It is with these two and with Dr. Holmes that Bunner is to be classed, I think—with the Locker who wrote 'At her Window' and 'To my Grandmother,' the Dobson who gave us 'Autonoë' and the 'Drama of the Doctor's Window,' the Holmes who told us of the 'Last Leaf' and the 'One-Hoss Shay.' They all three influenced him in the beginning; and so did Heine and Herrick.

And yet if the 'Way to Arcady' was inspired directly by any older poet's verse, it is not

Holmes's, nor Heine's, nor Herrick s, but Shakspere's—not the mighty Shakspere of the great
dramas, of course, but the Shakspere of those
lovers' comedies 'As You Like It' and 'Twelfth
Night,' the Shakspere of the sugared sonnets, the
Shakspere who was the most graceful of Elizabethan lyrists. Or if it was not Shakspere whom
Bunner followed when he sang 'Robin's Song'
and when he took his bell and cried 'A Lost
Child,' it was then those rivals of Shakspere who
wrote 'Drink to me only with thine eyes' and
'Come live with me and be my love.' For a
season or two Bunner's muse may have lingered
in Bohemia, but it was in the Forest of Arden
that she soon took up her abode, and there she
ranged the woodland in "the fresh fairness of
the spring." In the finest of the poems she
inspired there was an outdoor breeziness, a
woodsy flavor, a bird-like melody. A minor
poet Bunner might be, but he rarely sang in a
minor key. In his lightsome lyrics there was the
joy of living, the delight of loving—and I know
of no notes that are less common than these
among the lesser songsters of the modern choir.
As he wrote me when I was preparing a paper
on Mr. Dobson, the 'Autonoë' of that poet
"gives us the warm air of spring and the life that
pulses in a girl's veins like the soft swelling of sap
in a young tree. This is the same feeling that

raises ' As You Like It ' above all pastoral poetry."
And I think the praise is as applicable to more
than one of his own poems as it is to this lovely
lyric of Mr. Dobson's. " Our nineteenth-century
sensibilities," he went on to say, " are so played
on by the troubles, the sorrows, the little vital
needs and anxieties of the world around us,
that sometimes it does us good to get out into
the woods and fields of another world entirely,
if only the atmosphere is not chilled and rarefied
by the lack of the breath of humanity."

Coleridge hailed it as a promise of genius in a
young poet that he made a " choice of subjects
very remote from the private interests and circumstances of the writer himself." And this
must be my excuse for paying attention chiefly
to the ' Way to Arcady ' and its fellows rather
than considering the brisk and bright " society
verse " which Bunner also wrote with ease and
with certainty — ' Forfeits,' for example, and
' Candor,' and ' Just a Love-Letter.' But the
merits of these polished and pointed stanzas are
so obvious that they need no exposition. Yet it
may be as well to suggest that even here in the
" society verse," of which the formula is so
monotonous, Bunner had a note of his own; he
ventured his own variations. And his were no
hand-made verses, no mere mosaic of chipped
rimes. A gay spontaneity informed all his

lighter lyrics and helped to lend them wings.
His more serious quatrains, like 'To a Dead
Woman,' and the final four lines of 'Triumph,'
reveal no struggle for effect, no vain striving;
they seem to be inevitable.

To Bunner verse was perhaps the most natural
form of expression; and it is as a poet that he is
most likely to linger in men's memories. I think
this is the fame he would have chosen for himself, and I know how careful he was that his first
book of poems should contain nothing unworthy
of companionship with the best he had done.
The late Frederick Locker-Lampson once asked
Mr. Austin Dobson to make choice of all his
verses for a definitive edition of 'London Lyrics';
but when this was done, the heart of the poet
yearned over the poems Mr. Dobson had omitted,
and so these were then gathered into a second volume to be called 'London Rimes.' But when
Bunner had arranged the poems he proposed to
include in 'Airs from Arcady,' he consulted three
friends, and he omitted from the book every line
to which any one of the three had any objection
to proffer; and no one of the omitted stanzas re-
appeared in his next volume of verse—'Rowen:
Second-Crop Songs,' now included with 'Airs
from Arcady' in a single book of 'Poems.'

'Airs from Arcady' was dedicated to the friend
in partnership with whom he was soon to publish

a book of short-stories; but the final stanzas were inscribed ' To Her.'

> . . . Oh, will you ever read it true
>   When all the rimes are ended—
> How much of Hope, of Love, of You,
>   With every verse is blended? . . .

And a little while before the 'Midge' was published he was happily wedded To Her; and the dedication of every successive book of his to A. L. B. testified to the perfect happiness he found in his married life.   In time children were born to him, and three of them survived him. Two of them died in infancy, and it was not long after one of these bereavements that 'Rowen' was published, with these lines appended to the customary inscription:

To A. L. B.

> I put your rose within our baby's hand,
> To bear back with him into Baby-land;
> *Your* rose—you grew it.   O my ever dear,
> What roses you have grown me, year by year!
> Your lover finds no path too hard to go
> While your love's roses round about him blow.

(1896)

VIII

LITERATURE AS A PROFESSION

[This address was delivered before the Federation of Graduate Clubs, at Columbia University, December 28, 1899.]

LITERATURE AS A PROFESSION

THE best basis for a profitable discussion is nearly always to be found in an early agreement in regard to the exact meaning of the words we intend to use; and in any inquiry into literature as a profession we had better begin by trying to find out just what meaning we wish to give to each of the words thus united. To define a *profession* is easy. A profession is the calling or occupation which one professes to follow and by which one gets one's living. To define *literature* is not easy; for the word is strangely various, meaning all things to all men, calling for one interpretation to-day and for another to-morrow. But with the aid of the dictionary we may hit on a rough-and-ready definition not unfit for our present needs. Literature, then, is the communication of facts, ideas, and emotions by means of books. If we combine these definitions we see that the profession of literature is the calling of those who support themselves by the communication of facts, ideas, and emotions through the medium of books.

No searching examination guards the entrance to the profession of literature, and no special diploma is demanded of those who wish to practise it. Unlike medicine and the law, literature seems to call for no particular schooling. Apparently, the possession of pen and ink and paper is enough; and the practitioner is then free to communicate by means of books whatever facts, ideas, and emotions he may happen to have stored within him ready for distribution to the world at large. Every one of us is more or less trained in speaking, which is the earliest of the arts of expression — as writing is one of the later; and to do with the hand what we are accustomed to do with the tongue seems as if it ought not to be a feat of exceeding difficulty. Perhaps this apparent ease of accomplishment is one of the reasons why literature has only recently got itself recognized as a profession. Congreve and Horace Walpole and Byron all affected to look down on the writings by which alone they are remembered to-day.

Even now the boundaries of the profession of literature are not a little vague. Is a college professor a man of letters? Is a lecturer? Is an editor? And, more particularly, is a journalist a literary man? Any one who is thrown much with young men about to make the choice of a calling is aware that much confusion exists in their minds between literature and journalism; and they will talk of "going into literature" when what they really propose to do is to get on a newspaper. Even when they do perceive some difference between literature and journalism, they are inclined to hold that although it may be journalism to write for a daily or a weekly paper, yet to write for a monthly magazine is "to contribute to literature." But it ought to be obvious that this is a distinction without a difference, and altogether misleading. The articles dealing with temporary themes so frequently found in the monthlies are frankly journalistic in their intent; and as emphatically literary are certain memorable poems first printed in the dailies — Drake's 'American Flag,' for instance, originally published in the New York *Evening Post*, Holmes's 'Old Ironsides,' sent to the Boston *Advertiser*, and Mr. Kipling's 'Recessional,' written for the London *Times*. And just as these genuine contributions to literature appeared first in newspapers, so mere journalism very often nowadays gets itself bound into books — the war correspondent's letters from the front, for example, and the descriptive reporting that enlivens our magazines.

Far deeper than any classification of periodicals — the daily and the weekly in a lower group and the monthly in a higher—is the real distinction between literature and journalism. The distinction is one of aim and of intent; and there is a total difference of temper and of attitude. The object of journalism at its best is the opposite of the object of literature; and the two arts are in reality incompatible and almost hostile the one to the other. The work of the journalist, as such, is for the day only; the work of the man of letters, as such, is for all time. Now and again, no doubt, what the journalist does survives longer than its allotted twenty-four hours; and, more often than not, what he man of letters does fails of immortality. But none the less was the one done in the full consciousness that it was ephemeral, and the other in the high hope that it might be eternal.

In so far as the journalist is a leader of public opinion, he seeks to accomplish his immediate purpose by arousing and by convincing his readers until they are ready to do as he bids them. His chief weapon is repetition. He says what he has to say again and again and again, varying his form from day to day, indeed, but repeating himself unhesitatingly and of necessity. He keeps on hammering until he drives his nail home; and then he picks up another nail, to be driven home in its turn by another series of incessant blows. In one article he touches only one side of the case, reserving the other aspects for the other articles that he knows he will have to write. He lives in an atmosphere of controversy, and breathes freely as though it were his native air.

He plans no element of permanence in his work, and, indeed, never allows himself to think of such a thing. As the origin of the word journalism implies, the journalist seeks only to be sufficient unto the day — no more and no less. The result of his labor is to be sought in a movement of public opinion, having its record, perhaps, on the statute-book of the State and even in the history of the whole country; but his work itself has perished. Horace Greeley is the most famous of all American journalists, and his was a daring and a trenchant style. But whatever may have been his share in bringing about the abolition of negro-slavery, not one of his assaults on the slaveholders survived to be read by the generation that followed his — a generation to whom Greeley was but a name and a legend. It is the essential condition of the best newspaper-writing that its interest should be temporary; and no sooner has the journalist done his work than he must expect to see it sink into the swift oblivion of the back-number.

The man of letters is almost the exact antithesis of the newspaper man. He seeks above all things to express himself — to give form to a something within him that is striving to be born, to body forth his own vision of life, to record once for all his own understanding of the universe. He toils joyfully, without haste and without rest, never quitting his work till he has done his best by it, until at last he knows it to be as perfect as he can make it, however dissatisfied he may remain with his final achievement. The object of his effort may seem but a trifle — a little lyric or the briefest of short-stories; yet he never relaxes his standard, believing that the Tanagra figurines called for as keen a conscience in the artist as the Attic marbles themselves. Though he may work swiftly when the mood is on him and the muse inspires, he is never in a hurry. And where the journalist writes every night what must be forgotten before the next new moon, the man of letters may keep to himself what he has done, even for seven years, as Horace advised; and in all that time he may bestow on it ungrudgingly again and again the loving labor of the file.

Thus we see that journalism is a craft, while literature is an art; and that the two callings are almost irreconcilable. The practice of the one often tends to unfit a man for the practice of the other. There are journalists, not a few, who have become men of letters, and there are men of letters who have gone on newspapers; but I cannot recall the name of any man who won equal fame in both vocations. Bryant was a poet who was also the chief editorial writer of a daily newspaper; and one of his biographers tells us how careful Bryant was to do all his journalistic writing in the office of the paper itself, leaving his own home free from any taint of contemporary pressure. And there is an anecdote of Bryant that illuminates the conditions of journalism. A friend repeatedly urged him to advocate a certain cause, and supplied him with facts and arguments in its behalf. Finally an article appeared, and Bryant asked his friend if it was not satisfactory — if it was not good. The friend responded at once that the article was too good altogether, too complete, too final, since Bryant had said in it all he had to say on the subject, and, therefore, would not recur to it again, whereas what his friend had wanted was that the editor should take up the case and keep on writing about it, day in and day out, until he had really aroused public interest in it.

In other words, iteration is an absolute necessity in a newspaper, if it wishes to guide public opinion. But in literature iteration is almost a form of tautology. For example, now that we have Matthew Arnold's essays collected in a stately series of volumes, we can hardly help being a little annoyed by the repetition of his various catch-words, although these were strikingly effective when the original articles were appearing, in a monthly magazine here, and in a quarterly review there. We feel that something perishable has been obtruded into what we had supposed to be permanent; and we see that even so accomplished an artist in words as Arnold marred the abiding beauty of his literature when he sought an immediate effect by journalistic means.

And as journalism is not literature, neither is editing. An editor, like a journalist, may or may not be a man of letters; but there is no need that he should be. There is no reason to suppose that a man of letters can edit, any more than there is to suppose that he can write for a newspaper. To edit a periodical, daily or weekly, monthly or quarterly, is a special art, calling for special qualifications having no relation whatever to the special qualifications which the literary artist must have. Some literary artists have been endowed with the double equipment, but not many. Poe was apparently one of the few men of letters who are also born with the editorial faculty; and it is related that whenever he took charge of a magazine its circulation soon increased. Dickens also was successful as an editor, whereas Thackeray showed no remarkable aptitude, and soon gave up the uncongenial task.   Although their fame as authors must have aided them as editors, what Poe accomplished with the *Southern Literary Messenger,* and Dickens with *All the Year Round,* is to be credited to their editorial faculty, and not to their literary ability.

There is an analogy between the executive ability needed by the editor of a magazine and that required by the manager of a theater.   The special qualification of the dramatist the manager is not compelled to possess, any more than the dramatist is required to have the special qualification of the manager.   He may have it or he may not, as it may chance.   Molière was brilliantly prosperous in the direction of his own company; but Sheridan lacked what was necessary for the successful conduct of Drury Lane.

Just as men of letters may be editors or journalists, so they may also be lecturers or college professors.   Emerson and Thoreau were lecturers; Longfellow and Lowell were college professors. But it calls for no argument here to show that lecturing is wholly apart from the main purpose of the literary artist, and that it is not the prime function of the man of letters to impart instruction. Only a few of the lecturers under the old lyceum system were men of letters; and in our universities now only a few of the professors of the various literatures are literary artists.   Nor is there any need that they should be, since the duty of the literary artist and the duty of the college professor are not at all the same.

If the man of letters is not a journalist nor an editor, not a lecturer nor a college professor, what is he? By the definition with which this paper began, he is one who supports himself by the communication of facts, ideas, and emotions through the medium of books. But if we insist strictly on this definition, we shall soon discover that there are very few who follow literature exclusively. Often literature is seen to be a by-product of other professions. Literature, pure and simple, rarely rewards its followers with enough to live on; and the most of them are forced to look to another calling for their bread, even if they can rely on literature for their butter. It is but a divided allegiance they can give to literature, and they find themselves compelled to become journalists, like Bryant; editors, like Poe; lecturers, like Emerson; college professors, like Lowell. They have positions in the civil service, as Wordsworth had, and Burns and Matthew Arnold. They are magistrates and sheriffs, like Fielding and Scott, or physicians, like the authors of ' Elsie Venner ' and of ' Marjory Fleming.' Perhaps they have inherited invested funds sufficient to support them without the necessity of earning money, as had Gibbon and Parkman.

At the present time there are in the United States half a dozen novelists, as many dramatists, perhaps an essayist or two, or a poet by chance, each of whom receives from his literary labors alone enough to live on; and there are probably twice as many in Great Britain. But for the large majority of the men of letters of to-day literature is still what it was in Charles Lamb's time — "a very bad crutch, but a very good walking-stick." For example, when the Authors' Club was organized in New York, in 1882, by seven men of letters, only one of them was then supported wholly by literature—a novelist who happened also to be the writer of certain school-books; and of the other six one was a stock-broker, one was the editor of a magazine, two were journalists, and two had private means of their own.

However few the men of letters may be to-day who are supported by literature pure and simple, they are not less numerous than they were yesterday. In our own language especially, the conditions of literature as a profession whereby a man may earn his living are far more favorable in the present than they ever were in the past. The extraordinary expansion of the English-speaking stock on both sides of the Atlantic, the swiftness of communication, the spread of education, the granting of international copyright, have all united to pay the author a reward for his work never before offered. Shakspere, at the end of the nineteenth century, would not need to be an actor to make a living. Neither would Molière, since we have also international stageright. And Homer would not be forced to go on the road giving author's readings,—in his time the sole resource of the epic poet.

Whether this will be altogether a gain may be doubted. It did not hurt Homer's epic that he was rewarded for reciting it at the banquets of the rich. It did not injure Molière and Shakspere as playwrights that they were also players; of a certainty it helped them. It is not well for the man of letters that he should be free from close contact with the rest of mankind. It is not the worst that can happen to a genius that he should be forced to rub elbows with the common run of humanity. If a poet was able at will to withdraw into his ivory tower, to sing only when the spirit moved him, we should be likely to hear his lyre less frequently. If a man of letters could claim his share of some philanthropic endowment for genius, many a masterpiece would be missing that has been wrought under the rowel of need and the whip-lash of hunger. Perhaps if Shakspere had not had to get his daily bread we might have had more poems — and no plays at all. Not always is it a man's best work that is done after he has won his ease and has only himself to please. The artist, literary or pictorial or plastic, likes to dream of what he would accomplish if only he had the leisure; yet this is but a dream indeed. Give him all the time there is, and what the architect is most likely to build may be only a castle in the air.

To get one's living by making the thing his contemporaries can relish, this is a hardship, perhaps; but, like other hardships, it has a tonic effect of its own. This at any rate is what every one of the great masters of literature has done; he has had to please the men of his own time. He may have wanted to echo Charles Lamb's humorous ejaculation, "Hang the age! I'll write for antiquity!" He may have believed he was working for posterity. What he had to do, after all, was to conquer his contemporaries, to wring pay from his neighbors, average men and women, keenly critical some of them, and others sullenly stupid. He had to go before the jury of the vicinage and win a contemporary verdict.

For it cannot be denied, strange as it may seem to some of us, that posterity never reverses an adverse decision. In the long annals of literature, there is not a single instance of a poet or a playwright or a prose-writer being highly esteemed in the centuries following his death who was not popular in the hundred years following his birth.

And by popular I mean that his work was enjoyed heartily by the plain people for whom it was written. We hold now that the foremost of the Greek tragedians was Sophocles; and in his lifetime he was the most popular of the three. We consider Shakspere as the incomparable artist of the Elizabethan age; and his plays filled the theater and drew in the groundlings better than those of any of his rivals. We extol Cervantes as the most pathetic of humorists and the most exquisite; and there were rival editions of 'Don Quixote' in all the provinces of Spain within a score of years after its first appearance.

Dante, Molière, Goethe, each in his own way, was enjoyed by the average man of his own time. It is true, of course, that we see more in their masterpieces than their contemporaries could see; for it may take a century or more to give the proper perspective. It is true, also, that we see more in their masterpieces than their authors meant to put there; for they builded better than they knew, as every man of genius must. It is true, again, that in their own day it was their more obvious merits that were quickest appreciated, not to say the more superficial, and that therefore they had to wait for later generations really to understand and to expound the full value of what they did. The groundlings liked Shakspere's plays, and the tavern-critics praised his sugared sonnets; but while Shakspere was yet alive no one seems to have suspected the vast supremacy of his genius. And as for Molière, Boileau alone was keen-eyed enough to have a glimmering perception of his overwhelming superiority to the other playwrights of the reign of Louis XIV.

Of course it is not every favorite of his own generation who survives to the next — far from it. The next generation has its own favorites, and it delights in the sacrificial slaughter of the pets of its predecessor. The affirmative decisions of the present posterity will reverse by the dozen and by the score. The negative decisions it will never reverse. Therefore if we want to hazard a guess as to the authors of our own time whom our great-grandchildren will be required to study in school as masters of English, we must pick from among the authors who are widely popular now. The laurels of most of the favorites of to-day will be withered and desiccated, no doubt; but here and there a leaf will have kept green and lustrous. One or another of the men of the present will be able to read his title clear and to take his assured place beside the masters of the past. And he will be chosen from out of those whose books are now selling widely, and not from those whom the mere critic delights to honor. In the galaxy of the gods and demigods of literature there will be found no star whose brightness was not hailed by the people at large while yet it was young.

What is true of literature is not less true of the other arts also. The merit of the masters is felt by the plain people often before the professed critic is open-minded enough to perceive it. And the masters themselves are careless of professed criticism. As Michelangelo said, the test of a statue was the glance of the public eye in the plaza. To say this, of course, is not to suggest that the masters ever sought a present popularity of malice aforethought — that they ever lowered themselves to cajolery and base flattery of the many-headed beast. They wished to express themselves, to deliver the message that was in them, to do their own work in their own way, with all the individuality which is ever a certain sign of mastery; and the plain people liked them for the humanity that was in them, for the breadth of their appeal, for their universality, at the same time caring little for their technic as such, and knowing even less. Why, indeed, should they care or know? The eulogy of crafts-manship is for the fellow-worker only, who cher-ishes the difficult secrets of the trade, and loves to enlarge his store of them. The wise artist never flaunts his tricks in the face of all beholders; he seeks rather to hide all trace of his processes.

It was a damning criticism of the late Steele Mackaye that Mr. Joseph Jefferson made when he
declared that Mackaye used his acting to reveal
his method instead of using his method to reveal
his acting.

It is well for the permanence and for the variety
of literature that the man of letters should not be
allowed to narrow his art to technic, that he
should be compelled to make a wide appeal, and
that he should rely for support not on the qualities
which professed critics praise in his art, but on
those which the plain people may freely find in
his work. The man of letters may have his heart
set on technic itself, and so best, if only his
craftsmanship is a servant of his interest in life,
and not a substitute for it. "Laborious Orient
ivory, sphere in sphere," is for the cabinet of the
collector only, not for the glance of the public
eye in the plaza.

It is the constant danger of the artist that he
may come to have only technic — that he can
command the art of expression, and have nothing
to express. His very skill then tends to make
him remote from the healthy, common mass of
men; it gives him a disquieting aloofness, and
perhaps even a vague insincerity such as comes to
those who deal in words rather than in things.
Literature cannot live by words alone; it is but
an empty voice if it has no facts, no ideas, no

emotions to communicate.   Men of letters are to be found in other callings partly because literature itself is but a doubtful support, and partly because in these other callings they meet their fellow-men face to face and hand to hand, and so have occasion to accumulate the facts, to clarify the ideas, and to experience the emotions which alone can give vitality to literature.   And this is why the professions that seem akin to literature—journalism and editing and lecturing—are perhaps less helpful to the development of the literary artist than the other crafts which have no relation to literature.

Bagehot gives as the reason why there are so many wretched books that the men who know how to write don't know anything else, while the men who really know things and have really done things unfortunately don't know how to write.   We can see the truth of this saying more clearly when we recall the genuine satisfaction with which we receive the books of the men who have done something and who — by a double gift of fortune—are able to write about the things they really know.   This accounts for the charm of the autobiographies of artists and of men of action — Mr. Joseph Jefferson's, for example, and Benvenuto Cellini's, the 'Commentaries' of Cæsar, and the 'Personal Memoirs' of Grant.

In so far as literature is an art it is its own reward; but in so far as it is a profession it must provide a livelihood. And here is the crucial difficulty of all the arts when they are also professions. For the artist works chiefly to bring forth what is in him as best he can, for the sheer joy of the labor, in frank gratification of the play-impulse which is deep rooted in all of us. How, then, can he take pay for that which is beyond all price? When he has sought to express himself, to set down in black and white his own vision of the ·universe, or of any tiny fragment of it, then all-absorbing to his soul, how can money measure the delight he took in his toil? Yet this which was wrought in secret and with delicious travail, the artist must vend in open market, in competition with his fellow-craftsmen; putting it up to be knocked down to the highest bidder, huckstering his heart's blood, and receiving for it whatever the variable temper of the public may deem it to be worth at the moment.

And why not, indeed? Shakspere did this, and Molière also. And shall any man of letters to-day be more dainty than they were? Cervantes did the same, and Thackeray; Hawthorne did it, and Turgenieff; and their art was none the less transcendent, and they themselves none the less manly. They were modest, all of them; and they never cried out that the world owed them a living, or that the times were out of joint, since they had not every day so gaudy a banquet as a stock-speculator on the eve of his bankruptcy. Each of them sold his wares as best he could, wondering, it may be, why he should be paid at all for that which it had been so keen a delight to produce. Hawthorne it was who declared that "the only sensible ends of literature are, first, the pleasurable toil of writing; second, the gratification of one's family and friends; and, lastly, the solid cash." And Stevenson insisted that "no other business offers a man his daily bread upon such joyful terms; the direct returns — the wages of the trade — are small, but the indirect — the wages of the life — are incalculably great." Thus Stevenson speaks of the artist at large; and as to the man of letters he maintains that "he labors in a craft to which the whole material of his life is tributary, and which opens a door to all his tastes, his loves, his hatreds, and his convictions, so that what he writes is only what he longed to utter. He may have enjoyed many things in this big, tragic playground of the world; but what shall he have enjoyed more?"

The true artist dreams of a remote millennium when

Only the Master shall praise us, and only the Master shall
    blame;
And no one shall work for money, and no one shall work
    for fame,
But each for the joy of the working . . .

Yet, if we can judge by the history of the past, it is better for the artist himself that this should remain a dream only, and that he, having worked for the joy of the working, shall then take his wages in money, like the rest of us. It is better that he should not be tenant-at-will of a separate star of his own, but a resident of this workaday world where his fellow-man has a residence also. It is best that he should be forced to face the realities of existence, and first of all to have the delight of his labor, and then to take the hire of which the laborer is worthy.

The profession of literature is not for those who do not relish its toil and who do not love it for its own sake. It is not for those who are thinking rather of the wages than of the work. Above all, it is not for those who have a high standard of wages and a low standard of work.

(1899)

IX

THE RELATION OF THE DRAMA
TO LITERATURE

[This paper was read before the Modern Language Association, at the University of Pennsylvania, in December, 1897.]

THE RELATION OF THE DRAMA TO
LITERATURE

THE invention of printing and the extension
of education have given immense influence
to the art of writing; and hence has come about a
tendency to judge the other arts by the principles
that govern literature. Rarely do we find a man
of letters who is not ready with his opinion of
the picture in the gallery, of the statue in the
square, or of the play in the theater; and frequently his criticism is purely literary, being
supported by no special study of any other art
than literature, and being sustained by no famil-
iarity with the principles of painting, of sculpture, or of the drama. Generally the man of
letters is lacking in appreciation of the individuality of each of these several arts, of the essential
qualities of each peculiar to it alone and therefore most relished by those who can recognize
this. In a picture the man of letters sees chiefly
the story, the sentiment, the thought: he has
little desire and little knowledge to weigh the

merits of technic, by which alone the various arts are differentiated one from the other.

The painters have long protested against any judgment of their work in accordance with the principles of another art; and at last they have succeeded in convincing the more open-minded of us that what is of prime importance in a picture is the way in which it is painted, and that its merely literary merit is quite secondary. They are not unreasonable when they insist that the chief duty of a picture is to represent the visible world, not to point a moral or adorn a tale, and that in the appreciation of a picture we must weigh first of all its pictorial beauty. Nor are the sculptors asking too much when in a statue they want us to consider chiefly its plastic beauty.

What has been granted to the painter and the sculptor, the orator and the dramatist ask for themselves: they request that an oration or a drama shall be judged, not as literature only, but also in accordance with the principles of its own art. And here the literary critic is even less willing to yield. He may acknowledge his own ignorance of perspective and of pigments, of composition and of modeling; he may confess that here the painter and the sculptor have him at a disadvantage; but he is not ready to admit that he is not to apply his own standards to the works of the orator and of the dramatist. On the contrary, he maintains that the speech and the play, if they belong to literature at all, are, by that very fact, absolutely within the province of the literary critic. He cannot see why that which the orator and the dramatist may write is not to be read and criticized exactly as that which is written by the novelist and the essayist and the poet. Indeed, it is almost a misrepresentation of the literary critic's attitude to suggest that he has need to maintain this position: for it is rarely even hinted to him that he is not fully justified in employing the same tests in every department of literature.

Yet nothing ought to be clearer than the distinction between the written word and the spoken — between the literature which is addressed to the eye alone and that which is intended primarily for the ear and only secondarily for the eye. It is the difference between words written once for all and words first spoken and then written — or at least written so that they may be spoken. When this distinction is seized, it follows that oral discourse is not necessarily to be estimated by the same tests as written discourse. It follows also that the speech and the play may be very good indeed, each in its kind, although they may fail to attain the standard of strictly literary merit which we should demand in an essay, a story, or a poem.

"Much of the ancient criticism of oratory," says Professor Jebb, "is tainted by a radical vice. The ancient critics too often confound literary merit with oratorical merit. They judge too much from the standpoint of the reader, and too little from the standpoint of the hearer." For a just estimate of the rank of a speaker, "the first thing necessary," the same authority continues, "is an effort of imaginative sympathy. We must not merely analyze his style: we must try to realize the effect which some one of his speeches, as a whole, would have made on a given audience in given circumstances." It is this effort of imaginative sympathy which Schérer refused to make when he sought to show that Molière often wrote bad French. Looking at some of the scenes of the great comic dramatist from a purely literary standpoint, the critic found many faults; but these blemishes to the eye when the words were read in the study were, many of them, beauties to the ear when the words were spoken on the stage.

The dramatist and the orator are bound by many of the same conditions; and one of these is inexorable: Each of them must please his immediate audience. The poet can appeal to posterity; but if the orator does not hold the attention of those whom he is addressing, his speech is a failure then and there, no matter how highly posterity may esteem it. The sermon accomplishes its purpose adequately if it moves the congregation that listens to it; and so does a comedy if it amuses the spectators that see it. If a speaker holds his hearers in the hollow of his hand while he is talking to them, and if he makes them thrill and throb with his words, then he has done what he set out to do, even if his words, when reproduced in cold type, fail absolutely to explain his success.

To affect his hearers is the first duty of the orator: to move his readers follows a long way after. That an oration should produce the same effect on both hearer and reader is almost impossible: so competent a critic as Fox declared it to be quite impossible. When a certain speech was praised to him, he asked, "Does it read well? —because, be sure, if it does, it is a very bad speech." This is a hard saying. Indeed, we need not hesitate to call it an overstatement, if we let our memory dwell on the oration of Demosthenes on the Crown, on Cicero's denunciation of Catiline, on Webster's reply to Hayne, and on Lincoln's Gettysburg Address. But, like other overstatements, it may serve a useful purpose in putting into strong relief a side of the case which few of us see clearly. Lacordaire, a critic of eloquence as competent as Fox, is in substantial agreement with him. "The orator

and the audience are two brothers," he declares,
" who are born and who die the same day."

Perhaps cleverness is the final adjective to
characterize Cicero; and certainly nothing could
be cleverer than the skill with which the Roman
rhetorician was able to meet the double demand
on the orator — if we may accept the suggestion
of the late M. Goumy. The French critic maintained that the circumstances of the political
situation in Rome made it physically impossible
that Cicero could have delivered the diatribes
against Catiline as they are preserved to us.
They are too ornate to have been extemporized
in the brief snatches of time at Cicero's command,
and they are too long to have been endured by
the impatient senate, restless at the crisis in the
affairs of the republic. As the officer of state
charged with the duty of discovering and putting
down a conspiracy, Cicero no doubt made
speeches to the senate; but what he actually said
then — excellent as it was for its immediate purpose — can have been but a hasty outline of
the successive orations as we have them now.
Cicero was a born orator and a most accomplished master of the craft. No doubt the off-
hand speeches in which he reported the result
of his detective work, and in which he solemnly
set forth the awful dangers menacing the com-
monwealth — no doubt these speeches were

vigorous and adroit, and aroused to enthusiasm those who heard them delivered by the impassioned consul. But, as soon as he had leisure, Cicero began to polish what he had said; and he did not leave it till he had made it what he would like to have said; thus combining the advantages of the impromptu with those of sober second thought — the wit of the staircase, as the French term it.

As we are in the habit of recalling only the orations which are endowed with remarkable literary merit, we are naturally inclined to attribute to this literary merit their effectiveness when spoken, instead of seeking beneath the mere literature for the purely oratorical qualities which alone can account for their original success. To this day we read with delight what Demosthenes said in Athens, what Cicero said in Rome, what Webster said in the Capitol, and what Lincoln said on the battle-field. But the Greek orator and the Roman and the two Americans were none of them thinking of us when they stood up to speak. Each of them was thinking of the men to whom he was speaking at that moment: he was addressing himself to those who were actually within sound of his voice and who were to be moved to action by the words he was about to speak. If he should accomplish his immediate purpose he would be amply satisfied; and if his sentences should also reverberate through time—this would be but a surplusage of reward. The primary appeal was to those who were listening then; and the appeal to those who may read now is secondary and quite subsidiary.

To set up the immediate effect of the oration upon the audience as the chief test of the orator may, to some, seem narrow. But in so far as a man comes forward as a speaker it is surely not unfair to judge him as a speaker. And the first duty of an orator is to hold the attention of those he is addressing—or else why take the trouble of speaking at all? Why not ask leave to print and be done with it? Why go through the empty form of appealing to the ear, when the real intention is to appeal to the eye?

Some of the finest orations of Isocrates were apparently never delivered; they seem, indeed, although strictly oratorical in form, to have been intended from the first to be read rather than recited; and when we remember how important a part in the development of Greek prose was played by Greek oratory, we may even question whether Isocrates is fairly to be reckoned among the orators. But some of the finest orations of Burke might as well not have been spoken, for all the good their delivery accomplished. Burke's speeches are an inexhaustible storehouse of political wisdom from which succeeding generations will continue to help themselves. But if we apply the test of immediate effectiveness upon the audience addressed, we are compelled to deny to Burke the rank of a great orator. It is not a question of the matter of his speech: it is a question of the manner of the speaker.

It is quite inconceivable that a great orator should put to flight those whom he wished to bring over to his way of thinking; yet this is what Burke did, not once only, but often. When he arose to address the Commons, the House emptied itself. He might "wind into his subject like a serpent"; but his fellow-members fled swiftly to escape the fate of Laocoön. He was called the "dinner-bell"; and his friend Goldsmith has recorded that he

> still went on refining,
> And thought of convincing while they thought of dining.

Mr. John Morley judges that perhaps the greatest speech Burke ever made was that on conciliation with America —"the wisest in its temper, the most closely logical in its reasoning, the amplest in appropriate topics, the most generous and conciliatory in the substance of its appeals. Yet Erskine, who was in the house when this was delivered, said that it drove everybody away,

including people who, when they came to read
it, read it over and over again, and could hardly
think of anything else." In other words, Burke's
greatest speech has the same merits as his 'Letter to the Electors of Bristol'; and, for all the
effect it produced, it might as well have been
printed with no attempt at delivery. And here
the kinship of Isocrates becomes evident; however superior the Irishman might be to the Greek
in splendor and amplitude and penetration, they
both of them lacked the first requisite of the
orator. This condition precedent to triumph
was possessed abundantly by Demosthenes and
by Cicero, by Bossuet and by Webster — men
with whom it is not unfair to compare Burke.

It has been possessed also by many men of far
inferior powers, lacking all things that Burke had,
but having the one quality Burke was without.
Who turns to Whitefield's sermons to-day for
counsel or for comfort? But the size of the
crowds that Whitefield attracted to hear him
was limited only by the range of his voice. Who
cares nowadays to shake the dust from off the
five volumes of Sheridan's speeches ("edited by
a constitutional friend")? And yet so potent was
Sheridan's speech against Warren Hastings on
the charge relative to the Princesses of Oudh that
an adjournment of the House was moved on the
ground that it had left such an impression that

no one could arrive at a determinate opinion; while Pitt and Grenville, after consultation, decided that Burke's speech on the Nabob of Arcot's debts was not worth answering.

This discussion of eloquence may seem to some a digression, or at least an excursus; but it is justified by the essential similarity of oratory and the drama, the two oral arts, standing on the same plane and to be judged by the same standards. For example, the position of Burke on the platform is not unlike that of Browning on the stage. We may see in Burke all the qualities of a great orator; but the fact remains that those whom he sought to influence by his voice did not listen to him eagerly. And we may discover in Browning the qualities of a great dramatist; but the fact remains that his plays were not able to hold their own in the theater. And, in like manner, we may parallel the vogue of Whitefield as a preacher with that of playmakers like the authors of the 'Two Orphans' and of the 'Old Homestead,' who are ready to rest content if they can entrance the playgoer, and who have no hope of attracting the attention of the reader.

It is possible to discover in more than one dramatist of high rank the same feeling of distrust for a play that reads well which Fox so frankly expressed for a speech that reads well;

and it is easy to adduce instances where the dramatist, having won the kind of success he sought, has been satisfied with that, shrinking from a publication of his plays which would permit them to be tried by purely literary tests. John Marston, in the preface to his 'Malcontent,' — which he printed only because a pirate had already sent forth an unauthorized text,— asserts that "only one thing affects me, to think that scenes invented merely to be spoken should be inforcively published to be read."

For the same reason, Molière was compelled to publish the 'Précieuses Ridicules.' He also wrote a preface, beginning it by saying that it is a strange thing for people to be printed against their wills. He does not affect to despise his comedy, for in these matters the public is the absolute judge; and even if he had had the worst possible opinion of his play before the performance, he ought now to believe that it is good for something, since so many people together have praised it. "But," he says,—and here is the pertinent passage,—"but as a large part of the beauties which had been found in it depend on the gesture and on the tone of the voice, I thought it advisable that it should not be deprived of these ornaments; and I found the success which the play had had in the performance so great that I might leave it there." Thus we see that Molière, having composed at the same time the words of his piece and the stage-business that set off and sustained the words, was wholly unwilling to present to the reading public his mere dialogue stripped naked. M. Coquelin, in his striking paper on Molière and Shakspere, has remarked that each of these great dramatists had thrown his plays alive on the stage, and did not recognize them on paper. For the authors, ' Tartuffe' and 'Hamlet' existed "only before the footlights. It was only there that they felt their plays bone of their bone and flesh of their flesh." Both Shakspere and Molière were accomplished men of letters; and both of them were also incomparable masters of the dramaturgic art; therefore nobody knew better than they how much of its most valuable quality a play must inevitably lose in its transferal from the boards of the stage to the shelves of the library.

All the great dramatic critics have understood this; and they have tried steadily to cultivate the "imaginative sympathy" needful to enable them to see a play as it might appear on the stage, and to seek always under the flowing words for the solid framework of the acted drama. But the merely literary critics are rarely able to look for other than merely literary qualities. Even Charles Lamb, with all his liking for the theater, collected specimens of the Elizabethan dramatists which revealed them abundantly as poets and only casually as playwrights. The application of Lamb's method to the greatest of all the Elizabethan dramatists might have preserved for us more or less of the familiar quotations in Bartlett: but it would never have suggested the possibility of a volume like the 'Tales from Shakspere.'

The true dramatic critic has discovered that the dramaturgic qualities are as special as the pictorial or the plastic, and that, therefore, there is almost as much unfairness in judging a play by the sole test of literature as in so judging a picture or a statue. Indeed, to measure a drama by literature alone is like trying to criticize a painting by a photograph alone; and it is not the best painting that is most completely represented by the camera.

M. Ferdinand Brunetière, tracing the epochs of the French theater, asserts unhesitatingly that a play is under no obligation to be literary. "The drama," he declares, "can, if need be, live on its own stock, on its own resources, relying solely on its own means of expression." He explains that while the epic, for example, and the ode must be literary, as a condition of their existence, a comedy has no more call to be literary than a sermon. This bold opinion of M. Brunetière's is only an enlargement of an opinion of Aristotle's. To quote from Professor Butcher's admirable translation: "If you string together a set of speeches expressive of character, and well finished in point of diction and thought, you will not produce the essential tragic effect nearly so well as with a play, which, however deficient in these respects, yet has a plot and artistically constructed incidents."

Thus we see that while literature may deal with words alone, while it may be a matter of delicate verbal adjustment only, the drama can get along without this refinement. The literary merit of a play is in what the characters say; for that is all that is spelled out in letters. The dramatic merit must be sought beneath the surface: it is to be found in what the characters do, in what they feel, and in what they are. "Hence the incidents and the plot are the end of tragedy; and the end is the chief thing of all," said Aristotle. And again: "Tragedy is the imitation of an action, and of the agents, mainly with a view to the action."

After these quotations from two dramatic critics, let me quote also from two dramatic authors. The first is from the 'Souvenirs' of M. Legouvé, perhaps best known to American theater-goers as the collaborator of Scribe in the authorship of 'Adrienne Lecouvreur.' M. Legouvé tells us that "the talent of the dramatist is a very singular and very special quality. It is not necessarily

united to any other intellectual faculty. A man
may have much wit, much learning, much literary
skill, and yet be absolutely incapable of writing
a play. I have seen men of real value and of
high literary culture bring me dramas and comedies which seemed to be the work of a child.
On the other hand, I have received from persons
of no great intelligence plays in which was to be
found a something nothing else can take the
place of, a something which cannot be acquired,
which is never lost, and which constitutes the
dramatist."

And the second quotation is from the younger
Dumas, from the illuminative preface which he
prefixed to his 'Père Prodigue.' After asserting
that the real dramatist is born, not made, Dumas
declares that dramatic effect is sometimes so intangible that the spectator cannot find in the
printed text of a play the point which charmed
him in its performance and which was due perhaps to "a word, a look, a gesture, a silence, a
purely atmospheric combination." And then he
goes on to say that "a man of no value as a
thinker, as a moralist, as a philosopher, as a
writer, may be a man of the first order as a dramatic author"; and, "on the other hand, for a
thinker, a writer, a philosopher, to be listened to
upon the stage, he must indispensably be provided with the special qualities of the man who

has no other value. In short, to be a master in this art, one must also be skilled in this craft."

The history of the drama has a long list of more or less forgotten playwrights, skilled in the craft of the theater, cunning in stage-effect, and owning no other superiority. But this drama-turgic faculty, which they had as a sole posses-sion, was also the gift of all the great dramatists, who had this in addition to their poetry, their philosophy, their psychology. Not intricate plot of Scribe's is more adroitly contrived than the 'Œdipus' of Sophocles; and no melodrama of Kotzebue's is more artfully constructed than the 'Othello' of Shakspere. Vision and insight Sophocles and Shakspere had, as well as subtlety and power — things unsuspected by the writers of the 'Ladies' Battle' and of the 'Stranger.' But the greatness of Shakspere and Sophocles as dramatists was due, first of all, to that same gift of play-making which was the whole of Scribe's possession and the whole of Kotzebue's.

It matters not how beautiful a building may be, if its structure is feeble and faulty; for then it can be neither useful nor durable. Strength must precede grace; and the dramatic poet must begin by being a practical playwright, just as an archi-tect must master construction. Whenever a poet denies this obligation, and shrinks from due ap-prenticeship to stagecraft, he surrenders his chance of being a dramatist. The stage of their own times is the platform upon which the real dramatists have always found themselves at home. Euripides, Lope de Vega, and Corneille did not retire into an ivory tower: they brought out plays to please the broad public. There is no more patent absurdity than the play that is not intended to be played — the closet-drama, as it is called.

This unactable drama of lofty poetic pretense is largely a development of our own day, although it may find a doubtful ancestor in the tragedy of Seneca. The Latin phrasemonger did not intend his pieces to be performed; and this is fortunate for him, as the fate is not doubtful of plays in which the deed is forever sacrificed to the word, and in which the heartfelt cry is suppressed in favor of the elaborated antithesis. Whether Browning and Tennyson and Swinburne had it in them to be dramatists, nobody knows; but nobody can deny that they are not dramatists as were Calderon and Schiller, as are Ibsen and Sudermann. However various their qualifications, they fail to reveal the most important of all — the possession of sufficient stagecraft to make the performance of their plays profitable.

It is in this ability to hold the attention of an average audience of their own contemporaries that the inspired dramatists stand side by side

with the uninspired play-makers. Poets they
are, but first of all theater-poets, in the apt
German phrase. Even to-day, despite the gulf
of two thousand years that yawns between us
and the civilization of Greece, we are gripped by
the inexorable action as the awful fate of Œdipus
is unrolled before us in the playhouse, and we
are dissolved in pity. And as for the sad story
of 'Hamlet,' were that performed in an asylum for
the deaf-and-dumb, there would be no fear that
the interest of the spectators would flag. There
is that in 'Hamlet' which the deaf would fail to
get; and no doubt this is what gives the play its
significance; but what they could take in by the
eye alone would reward them amply for the effort.
By whom was it first said that the skeleton of a
good play was always a pantomime? And whoever has had the pleasure of seeing the 'Enfant
Prodigue' has had proof positive that the drama
can exist without even the elements of literature;
for here was a play that made us laugh and made
us cry, with never a word spoken.

The dramatists themselves have never had any
doubts as to the relative importance of the theatrical and the literary elements in a play. To
them the skeleton of action is everything; and
nothing the verbal epidermis. In the preface to
the 'Marriage of Figaro,' Beaumarchais assures
us that when he had mastered the subject of a

play he saw the characters before him. "What they will say, I don't know: it is what they are going to do that interests me." And Racine is recorded to have told a friend that a new tragedy of his was nearly completed — as he had only to write it. Here, in Beaumarchais and in Racine, we see an incipient contempt for mere writing that came to a head in the advertisement of a New York theater a few years ago, wherein it was proclaimed, as one of the elements of attraction of a certain more or less comic play, that it was without "literary merit."

A rough-and-tumble farce, hastily knocked together by a variety-show performer, to satirize rudely some folly of the moment, is of more importance in the actual development of the drama than can be any string of soliloquies and dialogues, however poetic or polished these may be. The farce that pleases the people has in it the root of the matter: here is the germ of the real thing; while the drama for the closet lingers lifeless and inert on the shelves of the library. The influence of the unpretending popular play — the folk-theater, as one might call it — is far deeper and wider than most historians of literature have perceived. The beginnings of Molière's comedy must be sought in the French farces and in the Italian improvisations of his boyhood; and no one has yet worked out the exact indebtedness

of Victor Hugo and the elder Dumas to Pixéré-
court and Ducange and the other melodramatists
of the boulevard theaters, whose labors made
the path straight for the Romanticists.

The reason why this folk-theater was so soon
forgotten is simply because it lacked literature.
Its merits were not only chiefly theatrical; they
were wholly theatrical. These plays were act-
able, but they were not readable; and when they
ceased to be acted, they disappeared into dark-
ness. The instant that they were crowded off
the stage, they fell sheer into oblivion. The success of a play, be it tragedy or comedy, depends
upon its fitness for the playhouse and for the
players of its own time; but the survival of a
play depends on its literary quality. Only literature is permanent. As the younger Dumas goes
on to say, in the preface from which I have
already quoted, "a dramatic work should always
be written as though it was only to be read.
The performance is only a reading aloud by several persons for the benefit of those who will not
or can not read. It is through those who go to
the theater that the work succeeds; and it is by
those who do not go that it subsists. The spectator gives it vogue, and the reader makes it
durable."

Upon this side of the discussion there is no
need to dwell. Nobody disputes that dramatic

literature must be literature, although there are not a few who do not insist that it must be dramatic. The great dramatists have accepted the double obligation; and they have always recognized that the stage of the theater, and not the desk of the library, is the true proving-room. This double obligation it is that makes the drama so difficult an art — perhaps, indeed, the most difficult of all the arts.

(1897)

X

THE CONVENTIONS OF
THE DRAMA

[This paper is based on the notes of an address delivered before the Modern Language Association, at Yale University, in December, 1894.]

THE CONVENTIONS OF THE DRAMA

IN her frankly feminine and agreeably Gallic 'Notes on London,' Mme. Alphonse Daudet records her surprise at the strange spectacle of old ladies going to the Queen's drawing-room at Buckingham Palace with bare arms, and shoulders uncovered, and hair bediamonded, all in the broad daylight. In Paris personal decoration so sumptuous is reserved for evening, and for artificial illumination. On the other hand, in England men put on the white tie and the dress-coat only when twilight begins; whereas in France this garb is primarily ceremonial, and is worn on state occasions, whatever the hour of the day. It was in a dress-coat and with a white tie, and bareheaded under the summer sun, that President Casimir-Périer followed the bier of the murdered Carnot. Mme. Daudet also notes that she kept to the French custom, and took off her bonnet when she went out to lunch in London, only to discover that it was the English fashion for ladies to retain their head-coverings at a midday meal in a friend's house. When the late Philip Gilbert Hamerton brought his French bride to visit his British family, he put her on her guard on some points, so she relates: "I was told not to be always thanking the servants for their services (as we do in France) if I wished to be considered well-bred."

Thus we see that the social practices of the Gaul and the Briton are sometimes sharply opposed one to the other, although the English Channel is but a narrow strip of water. When we go as far as the Suez Canal, we find Oriental customs as arbitrary as the Occidental, and absolutely different from them. In the Orient a man wears his hat in church or in the presence of his superior, and he takes off his shoes. The women of the East veil their faces, even though their figures be ill concealed beneath a single floating and diaphanous garment; and they are wont to think the worst of the women of the West who clothe their bodies and reveal their visages.

It would be easy to collect other contradictions as characteristic as these; but here are quite enough to suggest that the differing customs, although everywhere enforced by the pressure of opinion, are often quite illogical in themselves. There is no inherent reason why a man should wear a dress-coat in the daytime or should not wear it; the French decide the question in accordance with one theory and the British in accordance with another. The decision having been made, there is in each country an unformulated agreement as to the proper course on all occasions. These conventions of society are subject to constant change, but while they are in force they are quite as powerful as the unwritten laws that govern our political actions. In public life, for example, there is a tacit understanding that no President of the United States shall have a third term and that the presidential electors shall not really exercise any choice of their own. Upon conventions like these the whole structure of society has been erected, and life would become immensely difficult were we to begin suddenly to question the countless implied contracts to which we submit ourselves unhesitatingly without having given them any consideration whatever.

Language is likewise a convention, whether spoken or written; and our accepted orthography is only a common understanding to use certain combinations of letters to represent the several sounds of English speech. The Morse alphabet of dots and lines is no more a matter of consensus than is the use of the Arabic numerals. Every art has its own language and its own picture-writing. Implied contracts, like those

243

that underlie the art of human intercourse, are at the base of all the other fine arts also; and not a few of the denunciations of artistic conventionalities we hear so frequently are due to an imperfect apprehension of the condition precedent to each of the several arts; they are the result of a failure to perceive the terms of the tacit understanding between the public, party of the first part, and the practitioners of the art in question, parties of the second part — an unwritten treaty which alone makes that art possible.

The infinite variety of nature can never be reproduced by finite means; and therefore art necessarily consists in the suppression of non-essentials—the decision as to what is essential changing with every art, with every artist, and with every subject. Life is so varied and so complex that the poet, the painter, and the sculptor must each of them select from the multiplicity of details before him those which will best suggest the whole. The movement of real life is eternal, and the play of light and shade and color is incessant; yet the sculptor is forced to accept monochrome and to renounce all attempt to reproduce actual motion; and if he refuses to subscribe to the convention which allows him to falsify realities by excluding motion and color, the most he can hope to achieve is some sort of mechanical waxworks. In like manner, the draftsman in black-and-white represents a marble figure or an ivory carving by tracing dark lines on light paper, thus calling up before us the real truth by a denial of the actual fact. The screen-scene of the 'School for Scandal' is seen by us only because in the theater one side of Joseph Surface's library has been removed, the playgoers knowing that in real life most rooms have four walls, but none the less permitting the playwright to eliminate one of the four, or else he could never set before them what was taking place within doors.

The convention on which sculpture depends is that the statue of a living man may be colorless and motionless. The convention without which the art of black-and-white could not exist is that all the soft play of shifting color which perpetually delights us in nature shall be represented by dark lines of varying sharpness. As art cannot reproduce nature as a whole, it must rely on the implied contract for the right to make the suppressions and the modifications it thinks it needs. Some suppression and some modification is absolutely necessary; but so willing is the public to let the artist have all the license he requires that it has often accorded privileges not at all needful. For example, in the processions painted on the walls of the Egyptian temples, the sovran was always depicted as of a stature considerably exceeding that of his warriors. This conventionality, not being essential, was only temporary. Certain other conventionalities are tolerated without objection even now, when they are imposed on the artist by the material in which he is working; thus, as marble is fragile, the sculptor working in it is allowed to stiffen a nude figure by the wholly gratuitous trunk of a tree and sometimes even by a frankly unexplained support of the stone itself; but this privilege is properly denied to the statuary who works in bronze.

In no one of the arts are there more legitimate conventions than in the drama; in none also are there more outworn and accidental conventionalities. To study these is to gain increased insight into the methods of the great dramatists. The artist is rarely a theorist also; and generally he employs without question the conventions he finds in use by the predecessors whose apprentice he was. The essential conventions underlying the drama are permanent, like those supporting each of the other arts; and the playgoer is so accustomed to these that he takes them for granted and never cavils at the artistic deviation from complexity of real life. In the drama, as in the novel and in narrative verse, the author needs to disentangle the action he has chosen to set forth from out the countless accessory incidents with which it would be inter-mingled inextricably were it a true story. He needs to acquaint his auditors with that part of his plot which has taken place before the play begins. He needs to present his characters clearly and unhesitatingly, so that the spectator can follow them without confusion or doubt, perceiving at once the motive for their respective actions. He needs to remember always that his minutes are few and that he has none to spare, so that he must pick his words and compact his dialogue, presenting in a quarter of an hour a discussion that in reality might have been pro-tracted through half a day or half a year.

These are among the permanent and essential conventions, as necessary in Athens of old as in New York now. And by the side of these the student of stage-history can draw up a list of temporary conventionalities, acceptable some-where for a season, but seeming very absurd where they are not in fashion. In the Japanese theater the gorgeously costumed characters are accompanied each by an attendant in somber black, who is supposed to be invisible, and whose duty it is to hold his master's fan or sword and to act as his body-servant. In the Chinese thea-ter in New York, half a dozen chairs piled on the top of a couple of tables serve to suggest a moun-tain covered with ice and snow. In the passion-play, which still survives in New Mexico, almost four centuries after the Spanish brought it across the Atlantic, the Devil is now represented always in the uniform of a United States cavalry officer; and when Captain Bourke once proffered an infantry uniform instead, it was declined. In the Greek theater two thousand years ago, when a murder had been committed behind closed doors, the portals were opened from within, and there was thrust forward the *ekkyklema*, a platform on rollers, on which was a group — a *tableau vivant*, as it were — posed to represent the deed of death just committed out of sight.

Now, each of these spectacles seems to us unnatural and ridiculous; but no one of them so impressed the spectators before whom it was produced. Because they were accustomed to it and knew nothing else, it seemed to them perfectly natural. And this is not merely because they were barbarians or Greeks, since we New-Yorkers of the nineteenth century now accept as normal conventionalities which would strike a Chinaman or a Mexican, a Japanese or an Athenian, as inexpressibly ludicrous. Is the invisble attendant in black much more impossible than our stage waiting-maid, with her silk stockings, short skirts, beribboned cap, and bejeweled ears ? Is the frozen peak made of obvious chairs and tables much more impossible than the sudden lowering from the sky of a drop-scene on which is painted a street of solidly built stone houses? Is the *ekkyklema* much more impossible than our equivalent device of a wall made of wire-gauze and becoming unexpectedly transparent when the lights are lowered in front of it and turned up behind?

If we take time to think, we can see that these things are out of nature; but we are so accustomed to them that we accept them as a matter of course. So in other countries and at other times other conventionalities have passed unperceived, however abnormal and freakish they may seem now to us. The Greeks saw nothing out of the way in a tragic hero raised up on tall buskins and speaking through the mouth of a mask, which had to retain its set expression throughout the play, however startling the unexpected turns of the plot. The Latins found pleasure in a lyric monologue (called *cantica*) chanted by a singer in a corner of the stage, while the actor in the center made the appropriate gestures; and this has a modern parallel in our unsuspicious enjoyment of the orchestral accompaniment of a song supposed to be sung under circumstances where no orchestra could possibly be present — in the Forest of Arden, for instance. The English under Elizabeth expected to be forewarned of the exit of an important character by a riming couplet at the end of his speech, that they might be ready with their applause. The French under Louis XIV were not shocked by the presence of rows of courtiers seated down each side of the stage and leaving only a contracted space in the center for the characters of the comedy to transact their most private affairs.

As we read down the history of the drama we discover that almost every generation has prided itself on getting closer to nature than its predecessor did; but an analysis of this boasted progress shows us that it has consisted generally in the discarding of some of the more flagrant conventionalities of the earlier generation — for which others quite as arbitrary were often substituted promptly. A conventionality which had its origin in some circumstance of a single theater is transplanted to other theaters where it is quite meaningless; and there it lingers long, for the stage is the most conservative of all human institutions, very loath to give up anything which has once pleased the public. The Theater of Dionysus at Athens was the model of the Greek theaters elsewhere; and as it was so situated that the city was west of its stage and the open country east, a habit sprang up for a character to enter by the western entrance if he was a resident of the place where the scene was laid or if he came from the harbor, and by the eastern if he was a traveler by land. This Athenian custom spread to the other Greek theaters, where it was a pure conventionality, not dependent on the relative situation of the city and the theater. Nay, more, like so many other traditions of the Greek stage, it was carried over to Rome; and in the comedies of Plautus we find that personages entering "stage right" are supposed to come from the harbor, while those entering "stage left" are supposed to come from the Forum, the former being strangers and the latter citizens.

Perhaps the fondness of certain actors to-day for the center of the stage is a survival from the time when no other position was adequately lighted. In the early days of the century, before the introduction of gas, the footlights consisted of half a dozen or more oil lamps, and the point where their rays converged was very properly known as the "focus." Here all important passages of the piece had to be delivered, since elsewhere the accompanying play of feature was not assuredly visible. It is told that when one of Kean's admirers complimented him at supper after a performance of 'Othello,' saying that in the great scene with Iago he almost thought the tragedian would strangle the villain, Kean answered, "Confound the fellow! He was trying to get me out of the focus!" Under the electric light the face of the actor can now be seen clearly in the most remote corner of the stage.

Other conventionalities have been abandoned as the modern stage has become more realistic. In the last century the "box-set" had not been devised, which frames in a room with walls and a ceiling. A baronial hall was then indicated by side scenes placed one behind the other, the characters appearing on the stage through the "first entrance right" or the "second entrance left," after apparently walking right through the walls of the house. The spectators never cried out against this impossibility as we should nowadays, because they then had never seen anything better. So far as we know, nobody ever commented on the practice of the elder Booth in 'Richard III,' who, when the time came for him to fight Richmond, walked to a side-scene and received a sword from an invisible attendant. This frank conventionality is not unpleasing; Richard was there to fight, and he did fight, and how he got his sword was an inconsiderable trifle no man need note in that moment of supreme effort.

Junius Brutus Booth's simplicity here is far preferable to Charles Kean's conduct in calling to the actor who played the Porter and who was crossing the stage, at a rehearsal of 'Macbeth,' to answer the dread knocking at the gate. "Don't hide that key in your hand," cried Kean, "as if it were an ordinary key! Let everybody see that it 's a key of the period!"

No doubt Charles Kean knew the temper of those who came to see him act better than we can know it now; but it would seem that only when Macbeth and Lady Macbeth were wretchedly impersonated could any spectator spare a thought for the material implement in that hour of awful suspense. It is a most artistic convention which authorizes the stage-manager to keep all the accessories of a climax as vague as may be, so that the attention of the audience shall never be distracted from the points of prime importance, the faces of the men and women whose souls are about to be wrung with anguish.

Whatever may be said against the three unities, the unity of attention must ever be respected. Mr. Jefferson has told us how scrupulous Burke and Burton were not to interfere with one another in the scenes they had together, each attracting the eyes of the audience in turn and each remaining passive (or, at most, expectant) while the other was speaking. In real life both characters might have been simultaneously energetic, but as the audience can give heed to only a single performer at a time, the one comedian or the other subordinated himself temporarily, with the result of intensifying the effect of the acting of both.

It may even be doubted whether the individu-
alizing of the constituent fractions of the mob in
the Forum scene of 'Julius Cæsar' (as that play
was presented by the Meiningen Company) was
not an artistic error. True it is that no rabble
had ever before been so well realized on the stage,
and that if we watched the many-headed throng
while Mark Antony was making his dexterous
appeal, we could discover how this phrase or
that won over the successive groups of the populace. But we could observe the crowd thus
closely only at the cost of a certain neglect of
Mark Antony himself, who ought to center all
eyes at that central instant of the tragedy.
Splendidly successful as the Meiningers were in
their histrionic exposition of the fickleness of a
crowd, their performance explained the long survival of the ordinary stage-mob, a mere operatic
chorus, almost automatic, moved always as one
man, and always leaving our attention free to follow the plea of the protagonist. This traditional
crowd is a simplification of the complexity of
actual existence — an artistic convention that jus-
tifies itself.

As the spectator has but one pair of eyes and
but one pair of ears, conflicting emotions that
might be expressed simultaneously in real life
must on the stage be expressed consecutively.
Only one actor must act at once, the others bid-

ing their time. Since — in the final analysis — what we seek in the theater is acting, everything else must be kept subordinate to the actor, suppressing itself so that attention may be concentrated on him. To lay undue stress on the accessories of acting — on costume, for instance, and on scenery — is to divert the mind of the playgoer from what ought to be our chief source of pleasure in the theater. In his Shaksperian productions Charles Kean took an infinity of pains to have every dress and every background and every property historically accurate — an accuracy to which Shakspere himself had never given a thought. The theater was not built to hold a platform for illustrated lectures on archeology and history: it was meant to contain a stage for the depicting of human struggle, so that the soul of the spectator might be purged by sympathy or lightened by laughter.

It is in matters of costume and scenery that convention is perhaps most convenient. Absolute accuracy in either is not requisite, even if it were possible, but only such approach to the actual fact as will not distract attention by its incongruity. To-day we should not be able to appreciate Molière's acting as Cæsar if we were to see him as Mignard has painted him in the part, with flowing periwig crowned with laurel; but under Louis XIV that was the conventional head of a hero, and any closer reproduction of antiquity would have distracted the attention of Molière's contemporaries from his performance to the mere accident of his make-up. As Macbeth, Garrick wore the uniform of a British major-general — perfectly acceptable in his time, when playgoers had not been taught to think about historic propriety; and in the same part, John Philip Kemble used to wear in his cap towering black plumes, which Walter Scott once plucked out to replace with the single eagle's feather of a Highland chief. In Talma's time in France, the play-going public was slowly getting to have a vague perception of the wide gulf between the ancients and the moderns, and yet when the great French tragedian first entered the green-room of the Théâtre Français as Cinna in what was meant for a toga, one of the actresses, shocked at this unexpected attire, cried out reproachfully: "Fi, Talma, you look like an antique statue!"

As with costume, so with scenery: it best serves its purpose when it is least obtrusive. The most accomplished scene-painter cannot give us real sky on the stage, or real daylight, real trees, or real houses. He cannot present the real thing; the best he can do is to represent it. And as realism can go only so far and no farther, it is not a question of principle, but a question of degree. All he is called upon to do is to suggest these things to us, and to refrain from any too flagrant solecism which might jar on our nerves and prevent our giving our minds unreservedly to the play itself. If he places a real tree amid the trees he has painted, it looks sadly out of place; and what is worse, it also recalls us from our voluntary illusion and reminds us of the unreality of its surroundings. In the nineteenth century we are so accustomed to the elaborately upholstered set, richly decorated and sumptuously furnished, that we should now resent the simplicity that amply satisfied our ancestors.

The Elizabethans asked no questions as to where the scene of a play was laid; they saw before them a platform jutting into the yard, and they gave their attention to what the men and women did upon that platform. In most of the earlier Elizabethan dramas the scene is laid on the stage — frankly on the stage; and whenever it is necessary for the audience to know just what part of the universe the stage is then supposed to represent, this information is promptly supplied by the text, as in Marlowe's 'Doctor Faustus,' for example. There was no need of the alleged placards declaring the scene; these would have been an obtrusion in the eyes of Marlowe's contemporaries, who never cared where the place was, so long as the play was interesting. These supposed signs are no more than the Victorian explanation of a need not felt by the Elizabethans; and they are not warranted by the passage of Sidney which is cited in support. In the Greek drama, also, I see no necessity whatever for any scenery. The Athenians were quite artistic enough in their tastes to make believe as much as might be necessary. In the 'Frogs' of Aristophanes, for example, the earlier passages are on earth and the later in Hades, but I do not believe that this change of scene was indicated by any modification of the architectural background. Probably Bacchus, on one side of the stage, stepped into a pasteboard boat — as little deceptive as the basket-horses of our childhood — and pretended to help Charon row across the Styx; and when they had come to the other side of the stage, Bacchus simply stepped out of his boat, and everybody knew that he had arrived in Hades. We must not read our modern demands into the minds of the Greeks. To us a device like this might appear too primitive, although in a burlesque — and the 'Frogs' is a burlesque after all — anything of this sort would be accepted as part of the joke. But we are looking back at the simplicity of the Greek theater with the consciousness of our own scenic elaboration; the Greeks accepted it as an immense advance on the still more primitive dance in the market-place out of which the drama had been developed.

And even now, when we have been sated with costumes and scenery and have trained ourselves to be very exacting in these accessories, we are perfectly willing to do without them, if only we are warned beforehand, so that we are not disappointed of any just expectation. Sir Henry Irving once took his company to West Point and acted the 'Merchant of Venice' in the mess-hall, on a platform draped with hangings only, without any pretense of scenery; and never was there a more effective performance, so I have been told both by those who beheld it and by those who took part in it. Mr. Edwin Booth once went to the theater at Waterbury to act 'Hamlet,' only to find that the trunks containing the costumes had all miscarried. At his suggestion, announcement was made from the stage that those who wished their money back might have it, while for those who remained the tragedy would be given in the every-day clothes of the company. Here was a more startling experiment than Sir Henry Irving's, but it was equally triumphant, for after the first few minutes of surprise the spectators ceased to be conscious of the clothes and gave their minds wholly to the play itself. Thus we see that even in these sophisticated times, when we are told that Shakspere is possible on the stage only when presented with every richness of scenic display and costly costuming, we find that one of his plays was acted at West Point with costumes but without scenery, and another was acted at Waterbury with scenery but without costumes. In each of these cases the audience was forewarned; and here we have the convention in its strictly etymological meaning of "agreement." It was a condition precedent of their enjoyment that the spectators should not notice the absence of scenery in the one case and of costume in the other; and the audience had no difficulty in keeping its bargain.

The public never cavils at what aids its own amusement, and when it wants to know what has taken place behind the scenes, it welcomes either the *ekkyklema* of the Greeks or the temporarily transparent wall of Sir Henry Irving's 'Faust,' freely permitting the dramatist even to contradict the actual facts, if that will in any way help him in his task. Indeed, the willingness of the broad public to go halves with the playwright and to make believe as much as he may ask it, has always been underestimated, I think. Just as the skilful etcher translates the light and shade of a human countenance by an arrangement of sharp black lines and presents us with a portrait we are quick to call lifelike, though in fact no man's face is surrounded by a sharp black line, so the dramatist is allowed not merely the liberties he absolutely needs, but a few more, for good measure. Some license he must have, since art cannot repeat or reproduce the whole of life; and after the permission is once given to vary from the exact and complete fact, what does it matter whether the variation be more or less?

If we give heed to the conversation we hear all about us every day, we are surprised to discover how slovenly it is, the most of it — how involved, how full of repetitions, how studded with broken phrases and with sentences that begin anywhere and end nowhere. Very rare is the man whose remarks will parse and whose conversation does not abound in restatements. When we write out from memory the turns of a dialogue in real life, we recall and set down only the significant remarks and those which led up to these; the insignificant words, the repetitions, the digressions, we suppress as though we had never heard them. Probably the stenographer in a law-court is the only reporter of human speech who does not cut out tautology and straighten out grammar. The most prolix and tedious of novelists has never dared to encumber any chapter of his most sluggish story with the half of the trivial verbiage that would have accompanied a similar discussion in real life. If this variation from nature — the convention of condensation — is necessary for the novelist whose pages are as many as he shall please, it is doubly imperative upon the playwright, whose minutes are counted. One reason why it is difficult to dramatize a novel is due to the different scale of condensation used in the two arts — a conversation that seemed easy and flowing in a story turning out to be too loose in texture in a play and twice too long. Stage-dialogue, when at its best, when it has most of the directness and simplicity of good talk, is very far from the laxity of every-day conversation. In Augier's comedies, in Ibsen's dramas, we are in a world where every character is quick to seize the meaning of what is said to him and able to express his own thought with the utmost brevity and without any fumbling for the just word.

Having signed the convention of condensation and having accepted the play in which no phrase is wasted and no time is lost, it is only a slight additional concession that Sheridan and Beaumarchais ask from us. In their comedies not only has every character a mastery of terse speech: he is also a wit. From the picked and polished sentences of Sheridan, it is but a short step to the rhythmic prose that Shakspere often employs; and from that to blank verse is only a little farther. And if we once agree to rhythm, there is really no reason why we should not allow rime also. Shakspere used blank verse generally, but he dropped into rime now and again, especially in his earlier plays; Corneille, Molière, and Racine employed the riming couplet. In the Spanish drama *asonantes* were used instead of ordinary rimes, but the metrical scheme was often elaborate; and Lope de Vega especially recommends the sonnet-form as excellent for soliloquies. To us who speak English, sonnet and *asonante* and rimed couplet are alike unduly artificial, while blank verse and polished prose are so familiar that they seem natural. But the English practice is a matter of convention, just as the Spanish is and the French.

In Shakspere's tragedies we meet a people whose natural speech is blank verse, and in Molière's comedies a people whose natural speech is the rimed couplet. In French light opera we find characters whose ordinary medium of conversation is compact prose, but who become lyrical in moments of emotion. In Wagner's operas we are brought face to face with a tribe who know no other means of communicating their thoughts and feelings than song; they are not singing as ordinary mortals may do by an effort of the will — they simply have never suspected the existence of any other form of speech.

And just as the convention underlying Wagner's operas (without the acceptance of which that form of art is impossible) is that of a race expressing themselves naturally in song, so the convention underlying pantomime is that of a race expressing themselves naturally by gesture. The characters of the ' Enfant Prodigue,' for example, are not deaf and dumb; they are not creatures deprived of the ability to speak; they use gesture freely and inevitably because they have never dreamed that there is any other way to converse than by signs. One of these conventions may be a little closer to nature than another, but all of them are sufficiently removed from the actual facts of life; and although we may not be disposed to relish all of them equally, all are alike legitimate in art.

Another essential convention permits all the persons of the drama to use the same language as the audience, no matter what their nationality may be. Not only Henry VIII, but Romeo and Juliet, Hamlet and Ophelia, Brutus and Cassius, Timon of Athens and Dromio of Syracuse, all speak English in Shakspere's plays. In ' Henry V ' the scenes in the English camp are in English, of course, but so are those at the French court, and even those when the princes of the rival kingdoms meet and confer; yet when Henry V woos Katharine she has only broken French to answer his sturdy English. We see the inconsistency here when it is pointed out, but it does not annoy us in the theater. If all the characters did not speak our own language we should not understand them. That we should be able to follow the story by taking in the words spoken is a condition precedent to our enjoyment, so we do not deny the implied contract the dramatist pleads in self-defense.

Shrill protests greeted Signor Salvini's first appearance as Othello with a supporting company of American actors; and yet this novel arrangement was only a slight elaboration of the ordinary convention. When Mr. Edwin Booth had acted Othello the tacit compact was that all the Italians of the play should speak English; and when he acted Iago to Signor Salvini's Othello the implied contract called for a Moor speaking Italian yet understanding English, and for various Italian characters speaking English yet understanding Italian. When Mr. Booth had acted Iago (speaking English) with Herr Devrient as Othello (speaking German), Frau Methua-Schiller was the Desdemona, and she spoke English except when addressing Othello, and then she spoke German. In the Sanskrit drama heroes and the nobler male characters speak Sanskrit, while women and slaves speak Pali — the vernacular of which Sanskrit is the more ceremonial form. Oddly enough,

a similar distinction obtains to-day in the theaters
of the New York Ghetto, where Mrs. Van Rensse-
laer recently "saw an operetta in which most of
the characters spoke or sang comprehensible
German, while the pronouncedly comic ones used
Yiddish."

It is an indisputable necessity of the acted
drama that the performers shall so pitch their
voices as to be heard all over the house, and that
they shall so place themselves on the stage as to
keep their faces visible from all parts of the theater.   These are both deviations from ordinary
usage, since common sense tells us that a man
does not discuss his private affairs in tones to
be heard by a thousand people; and the doctrine
of probabilities assures us that only a quarter of
the time would a couple face toward any given
point of the compass. Even when two characters alone on the stage whisper together not to
be overheard by other characters supposed to be
in the next room, they can but pretend to lower
their voices, since what they say must be audible
to the audience — or else why say it? Many a
critic, accustomed to blank verse and to the absence of the fourth wall of a room and to a hundred other conventions he accepts blindly, unconscious that they too are out of nature, has
refused to legitimate the "stage-whisper," the
"aside," and the "soliloquy," holding them to

be a little too flagrantly unreal. It is not to be denied that the aside and the soliloquy are labor-saving devices which some dramatists have worked hard. The easy convenience of soliloquy, by means of which a tortuous character can undeceive the audience while taking in the other personages of the play, has been too tempting to many a playwright. The conscientious dramatist has tended of late to get along without the aside and the soliloquy. The younger Dumas and Ibsen and Mr. William Gillette (in 'Secret Service') have proved that it is perfectly possible to eschew them both. Here the later playwright holds to a higher standard of technic than the earlier, just as Molière made us perceive Tartuffe's evil purpose without a single self-explanatory aside, while Shakspere had allowed Iago to unbosom himself freely to the audience in the intervals of his hideous machinations. After all, what is the convention underlying the soliloquy? It is that Hamlet, for example, is a man in the habit of thinking aloud when alone. Few of us would refuse to sign this agreement at the cost of losing "To be, or not to be." Few of us, on the other hand, fail to think that the permission is strained when we find Romeo overhearing Juliet's soliloquy on the balcony. Molière took this license as well as Shakspere, for in the 'École des Femmes' the Notary overhears the soliloquy of Arnolphe.

The more we examine the history of the acting drama the more clearly we see that convention is only a question of more or less, since more or less convention is inevitable in the drama as in every other art. Some conventions are essential and permanent, as we have noted in the preceding pages; and some are accidental and temporary. Of these last — which had perhaps best be called conventionalities — a few are due to the physical condition of the theaters where they arose, while others have come into being for reasons not always conjecturable now. While the temporary conventionality is acceptable, no one remarks its absurdity, which is obvious to every one so soon as it falls out of fashion. The conventionalities of one epoch often strike the people of other epochs as grotesque; and the wonder is how anything so gross could ever have been tolerated.

Although every convention makes art remoter from nature, what of it? Nature is not art: indeed, if it were, art would have no excuse for existence. What art does is to give us a skilfully chosen part so arranged as to suggest the whole. No one who enters a theater really expects or desires to be shown an exact presentation of life; and the spectators are ready, therefore, to enjoy the artistically modified representation of life. Essential truth is what the drama can offer us, and not a collection of the mere facts.

Professor William James, after reminding us how a poor child will make a doll of a rag bundle having only the vaguest likeness to humanity, remarks "that a thing not too interesting by its own real qualities generally does best service here." Playgoers are as willing as little children to make believe. Experience proves that a too close imitation of the external facts of real life tends to check this willingness. "Real tubs" lead straight to the "tank drama." The stage is the realm of unreality, and a real tree is not as natural as a scene-painter's tree. A true sense of artistic fitness prescribes that the real and the imitation shall not be mingled incongruously; the picture should be all of a piece and not a thing of shreds and patches.

Once upon a time a little girl had amused herself by dramatizing a horse out of a sofa-cushion; and at last she came to her mother and said, "Horsey thirsty." The kind parent went to the sideboard and poured out a glass of water for the imaginary steed. But this the child rejected at once with a finer sense of dramatic propriety, explaining that a "purtending horse ought to drink purtending water."

(1894-97)

XI

A CRITIC OF THE ACTED DRAMA:
WILLIAM ARCHER

A CRITIC OF THE ACTED DRAMA:
WILLIAM ARCHER

O F a truth," said Gil Blas, "if indeed there are bad authors, it must be confessed that there are still more bad critics." And the reverse of this is as true: if there are few good authors, there are still fewer good critics. A single glance at any list of the Hundred Best Books will show that the great critics are far fewer than the great poets or the great orators, the great dramatists or the great novelists. The reason is not far to seek: in criticism the gift of nature is not all-sufficient, as so often it is in poetry and in fiction. There are poets who have little besides their lyric gift; and there are novelists who have only their gift of story-telling. What the critic must have is the gift of insight: but he needs also an equipment not to be acquired without arduous labor; and he must add, furthermore, two precious possessions—sympathy and disinterestedness. These I believe to be the four qualifications without which preëminence as a critic is impossible

—insight and equipment, sympathy and disinterestedness. Macaulay was not disinterested, and Carlyle lacked sympathy; and these deficiencies are reasons why neither Macaulay nor Carlyle is to be numbered among the great critics. In so far as Matthew Arnold falls below the highest standard, this lapse is due chiefly to his somewhat inadequate equipment: he had read the best books only; and he had not a scholar's mastery of all the books good, bad, and worse in any single division of knowledge. Of course the prime requisite is the critical faculty itself; and this is no common having: but it is of little avail if its possessor has not also a memory well stored, a mind unbiased, and a heart open to new forms of truth.

Rare as the purely literary critic may be, the critic of the acted drama cannot but be rarer yet, since his task is far more difficult. The former needs to know the theory and the practice of but a single art, the art of the writer; while the latter has to be possessed of the principles not only of that art, but also of two others wholly different, the art of the playwright and the art of the actor. And his equipment is harder to attain also; for while the literary critic can take down a book at will to consider it at leisure, the dramatic critic soon learns that the mere perusal of a play is only half his duty, and that he has not seized its full significance until he has seen it acted. He knows that no true drama reveals its entire meaning in the library, where indeed its presence is often more or less accidental, but only on the stage itself, to fit the exigencies of which it was designed and executed. Just as the critic of painting, in default of the work itself, may make shift with an engraving or a photograph,—well aware that the reproduction in black-and-white can give him only the form of the original and never its color,—so the critic of the acted drama cannot help feeling that the essential spirit of tragedy or comedy may well escape him if he seeks to grasp it from its pen-and-ink symbols alone in lieu of that bodying forth by flesh-and-blood executants which the dramatist intended.

Thus it is that the literary critic can command the mighty masterpieces of literature at the cost of a month's subscription to a library; while the critic of the acted drama has to take what he can find on the boards from time to time, making the best of his chances, perhaps even dying at last without having had the good fortune to see on the stage more than half of the mighty masterpieces of the drama. So it happens that in few fields of literary endeavor has eminence been more strenuously struggled for or more seldom attained than in the field of dramatic criticism. As we call the roll of the centuries we discover the names of only two dramatic critics—Aristotle and Lessing—on the list of great writers bequeathed to us by those who have gone before. Among the citizens of Athens there was Aristotle alone to match with Æschylus, Sophocles, Euripides, and Aristophanes. Among the subjects of Elizabeth and James there was no single critic worthy of comparison with Marlowe or Jonson, with Fletcher or Massinger. In the capital of Louis XIV there was only Boileau to set beside Corneille and Molière and Racine—and Boileau, whatever his rank, is a critic rather of literature than of the acted drama. In Germany, just before Goethe and Schiller, came Lessing, the one modern who can withstand, without shrinking, an association with Aristotle. The Greek and the German are the two critics of the acted drama whose supremacy is indisputable: there is no third name to be placed with theirs.

In the first half of the nineteenth century the Romanticist revolt changed the face of French literature, and made ready for the Realistic movement that followed in the second half of the century. Hugo and Dumas, Musset and George Sand, were followed in due season by Augier and Dumas *fils*, by Daudet and Maupassant, by M. Zola and M. Bourget. And the French have had three critics who hold their own beside these poets and dramatists and novelists—Sainte-Beuve and Taine and M. Brunetière.   Although all three have shown an interest in the theater and an understanding of the principles of the dramaturgic art, no one of them dedicated himself chiefly to dramatic criticism.   The more notable French dramatic critics of the century have been the pedantic Geffroy, the picturesque Théophile Gautier (who lacked any real liking for the theater and who had but a loose grasp of its theories), the trifling and flippant Jules Janin, the solidly established Francisque Sarcey, and the brilliant M. Jules Lemaitre.   Of these, Sarcey has been by far the most influential, as he has deserved to be by his sincerity, his immense experience, and his common-sense acuteness.   Every student of the stage is his debtor for the skill with which he has analyzed the conditions of theatric success.   Even M. Lemaitre, individual as his opinions are, long sat at Sarcey's feet, and still accepts most of Sarcey's ideas.   It is true that, as Sarcey advanced in years, he naturally became a little less receptive and a little more unwilling to change his point of view.

In the literary history of England we find Lamb and Hazlitt inscribed as the dramatic critics of the early years of the nineteenth century. But it may be doubted whether either of them is really to be classed with Gautier or Janin—still less with Sarcey or M. Lemaitre.   Exquisite as they are as essayists, and in spite of the fact that both of them now and again wrote about the actor's art with abundant sympathy and understanding, they seem to me rather critics of literature than critics of the acted drama. They discussed the works of the Elizabethans as though Ford and Webster and Marlowe were poets rather than playwrights. In their own day the unfortunate divorce between literature and the drama had already taken place; and, therefore, they were not put to the final test of the true dramatic critic—the judgment of an unknown play by its first performance. Nearly all the comedies in which Lamb delighted, as also nearly all the tragedies in which Hazlitt saw Kean act, were old friends, seen often before on the stage, and read often in the study; so that both Lamb and Hazlitt were supplied with the standards of comparison which the critic of new plays must perforce get along without as best he can.

Little as the English dramatists of the beginning of the nineteenth century demanded criticism, those of the middle of the century called for even less; and yet in George Henry Lewes England had a true dramatic critic. A philosopher of wide range and keen intelligence, with ample curiosity as to all questions of esthetics, Lewes was also an amateur actor and a profes-

sional playwright. His little volume on the
'Spanish Drama' survives to prove his firm grasp
on the essential principles of the dramaturgic
craft; and his collected essays 'On Actors and
the Art of Acting' may be cordially recommended to all who wish to gain an understanding of histrionic methods. Indeed, the three
books which I should suggest to any one wishing to begin the study of the stage would be
Colley Cibber's 'Apology,' Mr. Joseph Jefferson's 'Autobiography,' and this collection of
Lewes's 'On Actors'; for all three of them, each
in its own way, set forth the same sound doctrine and with the same zest and *brio*.

Now that the nineteenth century draws to an
end, there is evidence that literature and the
drama, after their long separation, are to be re-
married at last. Perhaps we are witnesses
rather of the courtship than of the actual wed-
ding; but we need no longer fear that any one
will forbid the banns. This conjuncture makes
the task of the critic at once more difficult
and more necessary. Fortunately, the occasion
called forth the man it required, in the person of
Mr. William Archer, who is generally recognized
as the foremost critic of the acted drama now
using our language.

It is a good sign for the future of our stage
that the English-speaking dramatists have now

begun to publish their plays; for it is a proof that they are no longer satisfied with the applause of the spectator, but desire also the approval of the reader. Upon the dramatist lies the heavy burden that he ought to be able to support a double test—first, that of the theater, and second, that of the closet; and this also opens for him a double opportunity. With infrequent exceptions, the dramatic authors of France and of Germany have published their plays; and at last the dramatic authors of Great Britain and the United States are following this excellent example. So long as the plays themselves could be seen only on the stage, and so long as they became but memories as soon as they were taken from the boards, there was little call for any collection of the criticisms these plays had evoked. Now that the plays are in our hands to read, it is well that the most competent of contemporary critics should republish also his record and analysis of the impression they made upon him when they were acted in the theater.

The half-dozen annual volumes of the 'Theatrical World' in which Mr. Archer has collected his current comment on the acted drama of successive years are not only invaluable to the future inquirer into the conditions of the theater at the end of the nineteenth century, but are also intensely interesting in themselves. Indeed, Mr. Archer's interest in the stage is contagious; and he can communicate it to his readers—except to such as may chance to be immune because of congenital distaste for the drama. And here he is rather like Sarcey than like M. Lemaitre, who is a little too detached and dilettante. Mr. Archer has a shrewdness, a logic, a scholarly wit, and a flashing alertness not unlike M. Lemaitre's, but he has also the deep love of the theater, in all its phases, which inspires Sarcey, and which makes them both take the stage seriously. At bottom Sarcey and Mr. Archer hold the theater as one of the most important manifestations of human energy. So, no doubt, does M. Lemaitre; but his Renanism leads him a little to question whether anything human can be very important. Moreover, while M. Lemaitre is sometimes tempted to take the play he has under consideration merely as a text for brilliant disquisition on whichever of the broader problems of existence it may chance to suggest to him, Mr. Archer is like Sarcey in preferring to judge a play first of all as a play, with due regard to its technic, discussing its message chiefly when such a debate is made necessary by the author's treatment of his theme.

The French are the most accomplished critics of modern Europe; and their preëminence is perhaps more obvious in dramatic than in any other criticism—the drama being the department of literature in which they have always been seen to best advantage. Therefore, to compare Mr. Archer with the two foremost French critics of the acted drama is to pay him a high compliment; but it is a comparison he has no reason to fear. His experience in the theater—and nowhere else does mere experience count for so much—is, of course, not so long as Sarcey's; but it is far wider. The French critic knows only the stage of his own language; whereas the English critic knows not only the stage of his own language (in Great Britain and the United States), but that of France, of Germany, of Italy, and of Scandinavia. And whereas both Sarcey and M. Lemaitre are a little parochial in their patriotism, Mr. Archer is wholly without insularity. He is cosmopolitan in his outlook; and, so far from resenting a foreign flavor in a foreign play, he relishes it keenly and savors the tang of it.

Perhaps the explanation of this may partly lie in the fact that Mr. Archer is a Scotchman and not an Englishman. It is England which is the stronghold of the Tories, while Scotland and Ireland and Wales are more liberal, not only in their opinions, but also in their social organization. Caste is still dominant in England: Scotland is more democratic in its structure. It was in England that Sir Aubrey de Vere found those extreme Tories who, as he phrased it, wished "to uninvent printing and to undiscover America." In more ways than one are the Scotch like the Yankees; and here perhaps we can see one of the causes of Mr. Archer's open-minded hospitality toward American plays and American players. Certain of the conditions of life in Scotland are liker to those in New England than to those in England. The Scottish universities, for example, are more akin to the American colleges than they are to Oxford, that home of lost causes. It was from the University of Edinburgh that Mr. Archer graduated, being a belated contemporary of Robert Louis Stevenson, with whom in after years his friendship was close.

He studied law, and traveled; and then he turned to journalism. His beginning was obscure, as most beginnings are. He had to wear the mask of anonymity, which makes difficult any early recognition by the public. He emerged into the light with his first book, 'English Dramatists of To-day,' published in 1882, when as yet there was no sign of that revival of intelligent interest in the theater which was to come almost immediately, and for the coming of which his collected criticism was a preparation. Robertson's teacup-and-saucer comediettas had already been put on the shelf; Boucicault's twice-told plots had already worn out their welcome; and the blank verse of Wills and Mr. Gilbert did not furnish a hearty meal for an English critic keen set at the sight of the feast then spread before the French critics, who were called upon frequently to discuss new plays by Augier and by Dumas *fils*, by Labiche and by Meilhac and Halévy.

In 1882 Mr. Pinero was but a promise of the future; four years later he had become an accomplished fact; and it was in 1886 that Mr. Archer published his second book, 'About the Theater' —essays on one or another aspect of dramaturgic or histrionic art. In the opening chapter he dwelt on the advance made since the appearance of the earlier volume. In another essay he discussed the ethics of theatrical criticism. In a third paper he analyzed acutely the influence of the practice of acting upon the performer himself.

Perhaps it was this last essay which suggested to him the very interesting inquiry the results of which were published in 1888 in 'Masks or Faces? A Study in the Psychology of Acting.' Diderot's famous 'Paradoxe sur le Comédien' —which is an attempt to prove that Horace is wrong and that the artist must not feel if he wishes to make others feel—had become a theme of discussion. The foremost actor of France, M. Coquelin, had accepted Diderot's assertion absolutely, holding that "this paradox is the truth itself." The foremost actor of England, Sir (then Mr.) Henry Irving, in an introduction to an English translation of Diderot's dialogue, had denied its truth with almost equal emphasis. Here was Mr. Archer's occasion. He sent a set of questions to the leading performers of Great Britain and the United States, asking them when they lost themselves in their parts, and how and why and why not; and he supplemented the answers he received to this catechism of the comedians with a thorough examination of such further information as might be gleaned from the abundant library of histrionic biography. In his discussion of the mass of contradictory material thus collected, Mr. Archer proved the possession of his full share of Scotch philosophic acumen; and hereafter this solid work of his must be the basis of any serious consideration of the essential conditions of the art of acting.

Less important than ' Masks or Faces ? '—but calling for record here—are certain other of Mr. Archer's publications, some of them earlier and some of them later. He issued in 1883 a critical study of ' Henry Irving, Actor and Manager.' He planned and edited a series of lives of ' Emi-

nent Actors,' to which he himself contributed in
1890 an admirable biography of Macready—
admirable especially in the fairness and the fulness with which he treated the fatal quarrel
between the British actor and Edwin Forrest.
With his friend Mr. R. W. Lowe—to whom all
students of the stage are eternally indebted for a
worthy edition of Colley Cibber's immortal
'Apology'—Mr. Archer has also edited and
amply annotated three collections of the more
interesting dramatic criticisms of his English
predecessors, one volume of Hazlitt's, another of
Leigh Hunt's, and a third divided between Lewes
and John Forster (the biographer of Dickens, the
friend of Macready, and the enemy of Forrest).
As a translator Mr. Archer has also laid us under
obligation by Englishing the prose plays of Ibsen,
the short-stories of Kielland, and the critical
biography of Shakspere by Dr. Brandes.

Between the publication of 'English Dramatists
of To-day' and his undertaking of the investigation into the foundations of the histrionic art embodied in 'Masks or Faces?' Mr. Archer had
become one of the best known of English critics
of the acted drama. He had learned his trade by
that time, and was master of his tools. Although
he took the art of the stage seriously, he was
never pedantic or pedagogic in his manner, but
managed to be light and graceful even in dealing

with ethical intricacies. He proved early that he
was not one of the Scots who joke with difficulty; indeed, his writing is distinctly witty,
with the playful allusiveness natural to a well-fur-
nished mind. He already wrote admirable English, although with an apparent ease and absence
of effort that might not satisfy those whose ideal
is rather the steam-dried style of Pater or the
verbal mosaics of Stevenson. He had joined the
staff of the weekly *World* of London; and his
articles were thereafter identified by his initials.
Although the practice of contemporary journalism throughout the English-speaking community
still permits criticisms which are not warranted
by the signatures of their writers, there is a
growing conviction that an anonymous review
is almost as unworthy a thing as an anonymous
letter. Whether Mr. Archer is of this opinion
or not, his rapid development, when he was
allowed to speak for himself and in his own
person, is evidence in favor of the French system
of warranting an opinion by a signature.

Equally rapid was Mr. Archer's rise in reputation. Indeed, for a dozen years now Mr.
Archer's supremacy among English dramatic
critics has been indisputable. More than any of
the others has he the fourfold qualification of
the merely literary critic—insight and equipment,
sympathy and disinterestedness. More than any

other has he the threefold qualification of the purely theatrical critic—an understanding of the principles of three arts all closely related and yet wholly distinct, the art of the playwright, the art of the actor, and the art of the stage-manager.

Diderot wrote a 'Paradox on the Comedian'; but he failed to formulate what might fairly be called the 'Paradox of the Dramatic Critic.' By this I mean to suggest the double disability under which the dramatic critic must always labor when he is a spectator at the first night of a new play. Perforce he has to judge the play through the performance; and he has to judge the performers as the play may chance to allow them to evince their ability. More than once has bad acting betrayed a good piece; and more than once has excellent acting cheated those who were charmed by it into a belief that the play itself was far better than it really was. The critic of painting can take his place before a picture, and study it at his leisure; seeing it as it is directly, and not through any distorting medium. The critic of literature can read as carefully as he chooses, even turning back to reread when he thinks this necessary; and he has in his hand the book, complete in itself, making its appeal immediately and without calling in the aid of anything else. But the critic of the acted drama can perceive a new play only through the refracting lens of the first performance as that glides swiftly past his eyes. It is true that an intimate acquaintance with the theater, an immense experience of the stage, an ever-alert cautiousness, sometimes seem to enable some dramatic critics to develop a sixth sense, as it were, by which this double difficulty can be overcome; and in the surmounting of this disadvantage I know of no one who has been so fortunate as Mr. Archer —with the possible exception of Sarcey.

In the introduction to his 'English Dramatists of To-day' Mr. Archer pointed out that the drama in England was then flourishing as "a non-literary product," and that it did "not exist as literature"; and he expressed a wish that there might arise in Great Britain "a body of playwrights, however small, whose works are not only acted, but printed and read." And he declared that he did not, in his "most sanguine moments, venture to hope that this nineteenth century will witness its attainment." That was written late in 1882; and this paper is written early in 1899, not seventeen full years after: the nineteenth century has not come to its final year, but Mr. Archer's hope has been realized. It is possible now to buy and to read not a few of the plays of Mr. W. S. Gilbert, Mr. A. W. Pinero, Mr. H. A. Jones, Mr. Anthony Hope, and Mr. Augustus Thomas; and it seems probable that sooner or later we shall be able to purchase and to peruse those of Mr. Bronson Howard, Mr. William Gillette, and Mr. Sydney Grundy. To say this is to say that the dramatist has awakened to his double opportunity, and is striving to rise abreast of it.

In the bringing about of this uplifting of contemporary English dramatic literature no single influence has been so potent as that of Mr. Archer. As a translator of Ibsen, he revealed how a technic of a most skilful simplicity could be applied to problems of pressing importance. As a critic of the acted drama, he was unfailingly encouraging to every playwright who showed the slightest inclination to think for himself—or even to think at all. He was not intolerant of any type of play; nor was he hostile to any form of dramatic art, as any one can see by consulting the five annual volumes of the 'Theatrical World' in which he reprinted his weekly reviews of the London theater.

It is to the public rather than to the playwright that the critics owe their plainest duty. Their obligation it is not to give advice to the artist,— for he is a feeble craftsman who does not know his trade better than any outsider can,—but to report to the possible playgoer what manner of play this is that has been produced, wherein it seems to them good, and what its blemishes are.

Only indirectly do the critics influence the artist
—by influencing the public, by creating currents
of opinion with which the artist floats unconsciously or against which he reacts sturdily.
As Lowell said, the force of public opinion is
like the pressure of the atmosphere: you cannot see it, but it is fifteen pounds to the square
inch nevertheless. To Mr. Archer, more than to
any one else, is due the existence of a sympathetic welcome for the efforts of a dramatist here
and there to step out of the beaten track and to
blaze his own trail. More often than not these
efforts are futile enough; but now and again
they do not fail—and even the failures are instructive and interesting to any one who is on
the lookout for the little cloud no larger than a
man's hand which is to bring the fertilizing rain.

In the main, Mr. Archer's criticism is sympathetic, although his sympathy is sane always
and never sentimental. He has his antipathies
also; as a Scotchman, he is probably a good
hater; but we find no protruding of petty ani-
mosities in his pages. Certain things in the
theater of to-day he detests; and he says what
he thinks: but he does not dwell on these things
again and again, losing his temper. He drops
on them a few words of scorching scorn as he
passes by, and then gives his time rather to the
things he likes, to the things that are worth

while. Here he is at odds with those who cry aloud for a slashing criticism that shall free the land of humbugs and pretenders and quacks. But he is in agreement with the practice of all the foremost critics of the past: he is in agreement with the formal theory of the foremost critic of our century. Goethe confessed that he was "more and more convinced that whenever one has to vent an opinion on the actions or on the writings of others, unless this be done from a certain one-sided enthusiasm, or from a loving interest in the person or the work, the result is hardly worth gathering up. Sympathy and enjoyment in what we see are, in fact, the only realities."

(1899)

XII

THE ART AND MYSTERY OF
COLLABORATION

THE ART AND MYSTERY OF COLLABORATION

IT may be said that curiosity is the only useful vice, since without it there would be neither discovery nor invention; and curiosity it is which lends interest to many a book written in collaboration, the reader being less concerned about the merits of the work than he is with guessing at the respective shares of the associated authors. To many of us a novel by two writers is merely a puzzle, and we seek to solve the enigma of its double authorship, accepting it as a nut to crack even when the kernel is little likely to be more digestible than the shell. Before a play of Beaumont and Fletcher or a novel of MM. Erckmann-Chatrian not a few find themselves asking a double question. First, "What was the part of each partner in the writing of the book?" And second, "How is it possible for two men to be concerned in the making of one work?"

The answer to the first question can hardly ever be given; even the collaborators themselves are at a loss to specify their own contributions. When two men have worked together honestly and heartily in the inventing, the developing, the constructing, the writing, and the revising of a book or a play, it is often impossible for either partner to pick out his own share. Certain things he may recognize as his own, and certain other things he may credit frankly to his ally; but the rest was the result of the collaboration itself, contributed by both parties together and not by either separately. To explain this more in detail calls for an answer to the second question, and requires a careful consideration of the principle of collaboration, and a tentative explanation of the manner in which two men may write one book.

I confine myself to a discussion of literary partnerships, because in literature collaboration is more complete, more intimate, than it is in the other arts. When an architect aids a sculptor, when Mr. Stamford White, for instance, plans the mounting of the 'Lincoln' or the 'Farragut' of Mr. Saint-Gaudens, the respective shares of each artist may be determined with precision. So it is also when we find Rubens painting the figures in a landscape of Snyders. Nor are we under any doubt as to the contribution of each collaborator when we hear an operetta by Mr. Gilbert and Sir Arthur Sullivan; we know that one wrote the words and the other the music, and the division of labor does not seem unnatural, although it is not necessary: Wagner, for example, composed the score to his own book. But no one is puzzled by the White-Saint-Gaudens combination, the Rubens-Snyders, or the Gilbert and Sullivan, as most of us are, for example, by the alliance of Charles Dickens and Wilkie Collins in the writing of 'No Thoroughfare.'

If the doubt is great before a novelet composed by two authors of individualities as distinct as those of Dickens and of Collins, how much greater may it be before books written by more than two partners. A few years ago, four clever American story-tellers coöperated in writing a satirical tale, the 'King's Men'; and long before, four brilliant French writers, Mme. de Girardin, Gautier, Sandeau, and Méry, had set them the example by composing that epistolary romance, the 'Cross of Berny.' There is an English story in six chapters by six authors, among whom were the younger Hood, the late T. W. Robertson, and Mr. W. S. Gilbert; and there is an American story happily entitled, 'Six of One, by Half a Dozen of the Other'—Mrs. Stowe being among the half-dozen.

Six authors for a single story, or even four, may seem to some a woeful waste of effort, and so, no doubt, it is; but I have found recorded cases of more extravagant prodigality. In France, an association of three or four in the authorship of a farce is not at all uncommon; and it is there that collaboration has been carried to its most absurd extreme. M. Jules Goizet, in his curious 'Histoire Anecdotique de la Collaboration au Théâtre' (Paris, 1867), mentions a one-act play which was performed in Paris in 1811, and which was the work of twenty-four dramatists; and he records the production in 1834, also in Paris, of another one-act play, which was prepared for a benefit of the Dramatic Authors' Society, and which had no fewer than thirty-six authors. This suggests an intellectual poverty as barren as that once satirized by Chamfort in Prussia, when, after he had said a good thing, he saw the others talking it over at the end of the table. "See those Germans," he cried, " clubbing together to take a joke."

For the most part these combination-ventures are mere curiosities of literature. Nothing of real value is likely to be manufactured by a joint-stock company of unlimited authorship. The literary partnerships whose paper sells on 'Change at par have but two members. It is this association of two, and of two only, to which we refer generally when we speak of collaboration. In fact, literary collaboration might be defined, fairly enough, as "the union of two writers for the production of one book." This is, of a truth, the only collaboration worthy of serious criticism, the only one really vital and pregnant.

Like any other partnership, a collaboration is unsatisfactory and unsuccessful unless it is founded on mutual esteem. The partners must have sympathy for each other, and respect. Each must be tolerant of the other's opinions; each must be ready to yield a point when need be. In all associations there must be concessions from one to the other. These are the negative qualities of a good collaborator. And chief among the positive necessities is the willingness of each to do his full share of the work. A French wit has declared that the happiest marriages are those in which one is loved and the other lets himself (or herself) be loved. Collaboration is a sort of marriage, but the witticism does not here hold true, although Mr. Andrew Lang has declared that in most collaborations one man did all the work while the other man looked on. No doubt this happens now and again, but a partnership of this kind is not likely to last long. Mr. Lang has also quoted from the 'Souvenirs Dramatiques' of the elder Dumas an opinion of that most delightful of romancers to the effect that when two men are ¡at work together "one is always the dupe, and *he* is the man of talent."

It is pleasant to be able to controvert the testimony of the great Dumas by the exhibits in his own case. Of all the mighty mass of Dumas's work, what survives now, a score of years after his death, and what bids fair to survive at least threescore and ten years longer, are two or three cycles of brilliant and exciting narratives: 'Monte Cristo,' the 'Three Musketeers,' with its sequels, and the stories of which Chicot is the hero—all written in collaboration with Auguste Maquet.

Scribe is perhaps the only contemporary author who rivaled Dumas in fecundity and in popularity; and Scribe's evidence contradicts Dumas's, although both were persistent collaborators. Of all the hundreds of Scribe's plays, scarce half a dozen were written by him unaided. When he collected his writings into a uniform edition, he dedicated this to his many collaborators; and he declared that while the few works he had composed alone were hard labor, those which he had done in partnership were a pleasure. And we know from M. Legouvé, one of Scribe's associates, that Scribe generally preferred to do all the mere writing himself. The late Eugène Labiche, almost as prolific a playwright as Scribe and quite as popular, did nothing except with a partner; and he, so we are told by Augier, who once composed a comedy with him, also liked to do all the actual writing.

In a genuine collaboration, when the joint work is a true chemical union and not a mere mechanical mixture, it matters little who holds the pen. The main advantage of a literary partnership is in the thorough discussion of the central idea and of its presentation in every possible aspect. Art and genius, so Voltaire asserted, consist in finding all that is in one's subject, and in not seeking outside of it. When a situation has been talked over thoroughly and traced out to its logical conclusion, and when a character has been considered from every angle and developed to its inevitable end, nine tenths of the task is accomplished. The putting down on paper of the situation and the character is but the clothing of a babe already alive and kicking.

Perhaps the unity of impression which we get from some books written in partnership is due to the fact that the writing was always the work of the same partner. Scribe, for example, was not an author of salient individuality, but the plays which bear his name are unmistakably his handiwork. Labiche also, like Scribe, was ready to collaborate with anybody and everybody; but his trade-mark is woven into the texture of every play that bears his name. It is understood that the tales of MM. Erckmann-Chatrian are written out by M. Erckmann and revised by M. Chatrian. I have heard, on what authority I cannot say, that of the long series of stories bearing the names of Besant and Rice, all that the late James Rice actually wrote with his own pen was the first chapter or two of their first book, 'Ready Money Mortiboy.' This assertion, whether well founded or not, gains color of truth from the striking similarity of style, not to call it identity, of the Besant and Rice novels with the novels of the surviving member of the partnership. Yet, if one may judge by the preface he has prefixed to the library edition of 'Ready Money Mortiboy,' Sir Walter Besant would be the last one to deny that Mr. Rice was a full partner in the firm, bearing an equal share in the burden and heat of the day. Comparing the novels of dual authorship with those of the survivor alone, it is perhaps possible to ascribe to Mr. Rice a fancy for foreign characters and a faculty of rendering them vigorously, a curious scent for actual oddity, a bolder handling than Sir Walter Besant's, and a stronger fondness for dramatic incident, not to say melodramatic. The joint novels have a certain kinship to the virile tales of Charles Reade; but little trace of this family likeness is to be found in the later works of Sir Walter Besant alone, whose manner is gentler and more caressing, with a more delicate humor and a subtler flavor of irony.

But any endeavor to sift out the contribution

of one collaborator from that of his fellow is futile—if the union has been a true marriage. It leads to the splitting of hairs and to the building of more than one hypothesis on the point of a single needle—surely as idle a task as any ever attempted by a Shaksperian commentator. I doubt, indeed, if this effort "to go behind the returns"—to use an Americanism as expressive as an Americanism ought to be—is even permissible, except possibly after the partnership is dissolved. Under the most favorable circumstances the inquiry is little likely to be profitable. Who shall declare whether the father or the mother is the real parent of a child?

It is interesting, no doubt, and often instructive to note the influence of two authors on each other; to consider the effect of the combination of their diverse talents and temperaments; to discover how the genius of one conflicts with that of the other or complements it; to observe how at one point the strength of A reinforces the weakness of B, and how at another point the finer taste of B adroitly curbs the more exuberant energy of A; and to remark how the conjunction of two men of like minds and of equally ardent convictions sometimes will result in a work harsher and more strenuous than either would produce alone.

For curious investigation of this sort there is

no lack of material, since collaboration has been attractive to not a few of the foremost figures in the history of literature. The list includes not only Beaumont and Fletcher among the mighty Elizabethans, but Shakspere and almost every one of his fellow-dramatists—not only Corneille, Molière, and Racine, but almost every other notable name in the history of the French theater. Cervantes and Calderon and Lope de Vega took partners in Spain; and in Germany Schiller and Goethe worked together. In Great Britain Addison and Steele united in the *Spectator;* and in the United States Irving and Paulding combined in 'Salmagundi,' as did Drake and Halleck in the 'Croakers.'

The list might be extended almost indefinitely, but it is long enough to allow of one observation —an observation sufficiently obvious. It is that no great poem has ever been written by two men together, nor any really great novel. Collaboration has served the cause of periodical literature. But it has been most frequent and most fertile among dramatists. We ask why this is—and the answer is ready. It is because a play calls primarily for forethought, ingenuity, construction, and compression, in the attaining of which two heads are indubitably better than one. And here we are nigh to laying hold on the root of the matter. Here we have ready to hand what may help toward a definition of the possibilities and of the limitations of literary partnership.

Collaboration fails to satisfy when there is need of profound meditation, of solemn self-interrogation, or of lofty imagination lifting itself freely toward the twin peaks of Parnassus. Where there may be a joy in the power of unexpected expansion, and where there may be a charm of veiled beauty, vague and fleeting, visible at a glimpse only and intangible always, two men would be each in the other's way. In the effort to fix these fugitive graces they would but trip over each other's heels. A task of this delicacy belongs of right to the lonely student in the silent watches of the night, or in solitary walks under the greenwood tree and far from the madding crowd.

Collaboration succeeds most abundantly where clearness is needed, where precision, skill, and logic are looked for, where we expect simplicity of motive, sharpness of outline, ingenuity of construction, and cleverness of effect. Collaboration may be a potent coadjutor wherever technic is a pleasure for its own sake—and the sense of art is dull in a time or in a place which does not delight in sound workmanship and in the adroit devices of a loving craftsman. Perhaps, indeed, collaboration may tend—or, at least, it may be tempted now and again—to sacrifice matter to manner. Those enamored of technic may consider rather the excellence of the form than the value of the fact upon which their art is to be exercised. Yet it may be doubted whether there is any real danger to literature in a craving for the utmost technical skill.

In much of Byron's work Matthew Arnold found "neither deliberate scientific construction, nor yet the instinctive artistic creation of poetic wholes." Accidental excellence, an intuitive attaining of the ideal, the instinctive artistic creation of poetic wholes, is not to be expected from a partnership—indeed, is hardly possible to it. But a partnership is likely to attempt deliberate scientific construction owing to the mutual criticism of the joint authors; and by collaboration the principles of scientific construction are conveyed from one to another, to the advancement of the art itself and to the unmistakable improvement of the mere journeyman-work of the average man of letters. For example, many even of the best British novels seem formless when compared with the masterly structure of any good French story; and perhaps the habit of collaboration which obtains in France is partly to be praised for this.

All things have the defect of their qualities as well as the quality of their defects. Collaboration may be considered as a labor-saving device;

and, like other labor-saving devices, it sometimes results in a loss of individuality. One is inclined to suspect a lack of spontaneity in the works which two authors have written together, and in which we are likely to find polish, finish, and perfection of mechanism. To call the result of collaboration often over-labored, or to condemn it as cut-and-dried, would be to express with unduly brutal frankness the criticism it is best merely to suggest. By the very fact of a partnership with its talking over, its searching discussion, its untiring pursuit of the idea into the most remote fastnesses, there may be an over-sharpness of outline, a deprivation of that vagueness of contour not seldom strangely fascinating.

No doubt in the work of two men there is a loss of the unexpected, and the story must of necessity move straight forward by the shortest road, not lingering by the wayside in hope of windfalls. There is less chance of unforeseen developments suggesting themselves as the pen speeds on its way across the paper—and every writer knows how the pen often runs away with him across country and over many a five-barred gate which he had never intended to take: but as there is less chance of the unforeseen, so is there also less chance that the unforeseen will be worth having. Above all is there far less likelihood of the writer's suddenly finding him-

self up a blind alley with a sign of No Thoroughfare staring him in the face. It has been objected
that in books prepared in partnership even the
writing is hard and arid, as though each writer
were working on a foreign suggestion and lacking the freedom with which a man may treat
his own invention. If a writer feels thus, the
partnership is unprofitable and unnatural, and he
had best get a divorce as soon as may be. In a
genuine collaboration each of the parties thereto
ought to have so far contributed to the story that
he can consider every incident to be his, and his
the whole work when it is completed.

As it happens, there is one department of literature in which the defect of collaboration almost
becomes a quality. For a drama deliberate scientific construction is absolutely essential. In
play-making an author must know the last word
before he sets down the first. From the rigid
limitations of time and space there is no room
on the stage for unexpected development. Voltaire tells us that there were misers before the
invention of money; and no doubt there were
literary partnerships before the first playhouse
was built. But the value of collaboration to the
playwright has been instinctively recognized
whenever and wherever the theater has flourished
most abundantly; and as soon as the dramas of
a country are of domestic manufacture, and cease

to be mainly imported from abroad, the play-makers take to collaboration immediately.

In the golden era of Spain, when Lope de Vega and Calderon were writing for the stage, they had partners and pupils. In England there was scarce one of all the marvelous company of the Elizabethan dramatists who did not join hands in the making of plays. Fletcher, for example, wrote with Massinger even while Beaumont was alive. Chapman had for associates Marston, and Shirley, and Ben Jonson. Dekker worked in partnership with Ford, Webster, Massinger, and Middleton; while Middleton combined with Dekker, Fletcher, Rowley, and Ben Jonson.

In France, a country where the true principles of the play-maker's art are most thoroughly understood, Rotrou and Corneille worked to-gether with three others on five-act tragedies barely outlined by Cardinal Richelieu. Corneille and Quinault aided Molière in the writing of 'Psyche.' Boileau and La Fontaine and other friends helped Racine to complete the 'Plaideurs.' In the present century, when the supremacy of the French drama is again indisputable, many of the best plays are due to collaboration. Scribe and M. Legouvé wrote together 'Adrienne Le-couvreur' and the 'Bataille des Dames.' MM. Meilhac and Halévy were joint authors of 'Frou-frou' (that poignant picture of the disadvantages of self-sacrifice) and of the 'Grand Duchess of Gérolstein' (that bold and brilliant satire of imperial misrule). Émile Augier, to my mind the most wholesome and the most manly dramatist of our day, joined Jules Sandeau in composing the 'Gendre de M. Poirier,' the most satisfactory comedy of the century.

Scribe and Augier and Sandeau, M. Legouvé, Meilhac, and M. Halévy, are all men of fine talents and of varied accomplishments in letters; they are individually the authors of many another drama; but no one of these other pieces attains the stature of the coöperative plays or even approaches the standard thus set. Nothing else of Scribe's is as human and as pathetic as 'Adrienne Lecouvreur,' and nothing else of M. Legouvé's is as skilful. Since the dissolution of the partnership of MM. Meilhac and Halévy they have each written alone. M. Halévy's 'Abbé Constantin' is a charming idyl, and Meilhac's 'Décoré' is delicately humorous; but where is the underlying strength which sustains 'Frou-frou'? where is the exuberant comic force of 'Tricoche et Cacolet'? where is the disintegrating irony of the 'Belle Hélène'? Here collaboration has proved itself. Here union has produced work finer and higher than was apparently possible to either author alone. More often than not collaboration seems accidental, and its results are not the works by which we rank either of its writers. We do not think of Charles Dickens chiefly as the author of 'No Thoroughfare,' nor is 'No Thoroughfare' the book by which we judge Wilkie Collins. But 'Adrienne Lecouvreur' is the finest play on the list of either Scribe's works or of M. Legouvé's, and 'Frou-frou' is perhaps the most likely to survive of all MM. Meilhac and Halévy's varied dramatic efforts.

France is the country with the most vigorous dramatic literature, and France is the country where collaboration is the most frequent. The two facts are to be set down together, without a forced suggestion that either is a consequence of the other. But it is to be noted again that in any country where there is a revival of the drama collaboration is likely to become common at once. In Germany just now, for example, there is a promising school of comedy-writers—and they are combining one with another. In Great Britain and in the United States there are signs of dramatic growth; and very obviously there has been an enormous improvement in the past few years. A comparison of the original plays written in our language twenty-five years ago with those now so written is most encouraging. It may seem a little like that circular argument,—which is as dangerous as a circular saw,—but I venture to suggest that one of the causes of

immediate hopefulness for the drama in our language is the prevalence of collaboration in England and in America; for by such partnerships
the principles of play-making are spread abroad.
"We learn of our contemporaries," said Emerson, "what they know, without effort, and almost through the pores of the skin." Now, a
collaborator must needs be the closest of contemporaries.

With Charles Reade, Tom Taylor composed
'Masks and Faces,' an artificial comedy of undeniable effect; and with Mr. A. W. Dubourg he
wrote 'New Men and Old Acres,' a comedy also
artificial, but more closely akin to modern life.
With Palgrave Simpson, Mr. Herman Merivale
prepared a moving romantic drama, 'All for Her,'
and with Mr. F. C. Grove he wrote a brilliant
comedy, 'Forget-me-not.' To collaboration
again is due the 'Silver King,' the best of recent
English dramas of its type. And collaboration,
alas! is also to be credited with the most of the
latest machine-made British melodramas, plays
which may bear the signatures of any two of
half a dozen contemporary playwrights—which
reveal a most extraordinary likeness one to the
other, as though they had each been cut from
the same roll of goods in lengths to suit the pur-
chaser, and in which the pattern is always a
variation of a single theme, the revengeful pur-

suit of an exemplary good man by an indefatigable bad man.

In America there is also an evident tendency toward coöperation, as there has been a distinct improvement in the technic of play-writing. Mr. Bronson Howard has told us that he had a silent partner in revising his 'Banker's Daughter,' known in England as the 'Old Love and the New.' To the novice in the theater the aid of the expert is invaluable. When Mrs. Hodgson Burnett desired to make a play out of her little tale of 'Esmeralda,' she consulted counsel learned in the law of dramatic construction, Mr. William Gillette, by whose aid the comedy was written. If the poetic drama has any future on our stage, it must owe this in a measure to collaboration, for the technic of the theater is nowadays very elaborate, and few bards are likely to master it satisfactorily. But if the poet will frankly join hands with the practical playwright, there is a hopeful possibility of success. Had Browning taken advice before he finally fixed on his action, and while the form was yet fluid, 'A Blot in the Scutcheon' might have been made a great acting play. It is while a drama is still malleable that the aid of the expert is invaluable.

The assistance which Dumas received from his frequent associates was not of this kind; it was not the coöperation of an expert partner, but

rather that of a useful apprentice. The chief of
these collaborators was the late Auguste Maquet,
with whom Dumas would block out the plot,
and to whom he would intrust all the toilsome
detail of investigation and verification. Edmond
About once caught Dumas red-handed in the very
act of collaboration, and from his account it appears that Maquet had set down in black-and-
white the outline of the story as they had developed it together, incorporating, doubtless, his
own suggestions and the result of his historic
research. This outline was contained on little
squares of paper, and each of these little squares
Dumas was amplifying into a large sheet of
manuscript in his own fine handwriting.

Thackeray answered the accusation that
Dumas did not write all his own works by asking, "Does not the chief cook have *aides* under
him? Did not Rubens's pupils paint on his
canvases?" Then—it is in one of the most
delightful passages of the always delightful
'Roundabout Papers'—he declares that he himself would like a competent, respectable, and
rapid clerk to whom he might say, "Mr. Jones,
if you please, the archbishop must die this morning in about five pages. Turn to article 'Dropsy'
(or what you will) in encyclopedia. Take care
there are no medical blunders in his death.
Group his daughters. physicians, and chaplains

round him. In Wales's 'London,' letter B, third shelf, you will find an account of Lambeth, and some prints of the place. Color in with local coloring. The daughter will come down and speak to her lover in his wherry at Lambeth Stairs." "Jones (an intelligent young man) examines the medical, historical, topographical books necessary; his chief points out to him in Jeremy Taylor (fol. London, MDCLV) a few remarks such as might befit a dear old archbishop departing this life. When I come back to dress for dinner the archbishop is dead on my table in five pages,—medicine, topography, theology, all right,—and Jones has gone home to his family some hours." This was Thackeray's whimsical suggestion; but if he had ventured to adopt it himself, I fear we should have been able to distinguish the prentice hand from the fine round sweep of the master.

This paper is, perhaps, rather a consideration of the principle of collaboration than an explanation of its methods. To point out the departments of literature in which collaboration may be of advantage and to indicate its more apparent limitations have been my objects, and I have postponed as long as I could any attempt to explain "how it is done." Such an explanation is at best but a doubtful possibility.

Perhaps the first requisite is a sympathy between the two partners not sufficient to make them survey life from the same point of view, but yet enough to make them respect each other's suggestions and be prepared to accept them. There is needed in both openness of mind as well as alertness, an ability to take as well as to give, a willingness to put yourself in his place and to look at the world from his standpoint. Probably it is best that the two authors shall not be too much alike in temperament. Edmond and Jules de Goncourt, for example, although not twins, thought alike on most subjects; and so close was their identity of cerebration that when they were sitting at the same table at work on the same book, they sometimes wrote almost the same sentence at the same moment. This is collaboration carried to an abnormal and unwholesome extreme; and there is much that is morbid and much that is forced in the books the Goncourts composed together.

Collaboration may once more be likened to matrimony, and we may consider MM. Erckmann-Chatrian and Messrs. Besant and Rice as monogamists, while Scribe and Labiche, who were ready to collaborate at large, are polygamists. In marriage husband and wife are one, and that is not a happy union when either inquires as to which one it is: the unity should be so complete that the will of each is merged in that of the other. So it should be in a literary partnership. Respect for each other, mutual esteem, is, perhaps, the first requisite for collaboration, as for matrimony; and good temper is assuredly the second.

In discussing the practice of collaboration with that passed master of the art Sir Walter Besant, he declared to me that it was absolutely essential that one of the two partners should be the head of the firm. He did not tell me who was the head of the firm of Besant and Rice, and I have no direct testimony to offer in support of my belief that the dominant member was Sir Walter himself; but there is a plenty of circumstantial evidence to that effect, and, as Thoreau says, "some circumstantial evidence is very strong—as when you find a trout in the milk."

What Sir Walter Besant meant, I take it, was that there must be a unity of impulse so that the resulting product shall seem the outcome of a single controlling mind. This may be attained by the domination of one partner, no doubt, as when Dumas availed himself of the aid of Maquet; but it can be the result also of an harmonious equality, as when Meilhac and M. Halévy were writing together. In collaboration as in matrimony, again, it is well when the influence of the masculine element does not wholly overpower the feminine.

As there are households where husband and wife fight like cat and dog, and where marriage ends in divorce, so there are literary partnerships which are dissolved in acrimony and anger. Alexandre Dumas *fils* has lent his strength to the authors of the 'Supplice d'une Femme,' 'Héloïse Paranquet,' and the 'Danicheff,' and there followed bad feelings and high words. Warned by this bitter experience, Dumas is said to have answered a request to collaborate with the query, "Why should I wish to quarrel with you?" But Dumas was a bad collaborator, I fancy, despite his skill and his strength. He was like the powerful ally a weak country sometimes calls in to its own undoing. Yet in his case the usual cause of disagreement between collaborators was lacking, for the plays succeeded which he recast and stamped with his own image and superscription. In general it is when the work fails that the collaborators fall out. Racine made an epigram against the two now forgotten authors of a now forgotten tragedy, that each claimed it before it was produced and both renounced it after it had been acted.

If I may be allowed to offer myself as a witness, I shall testify to the advantage of a literary partnership which halves the labor of the task and doubles the pleasure. It may be that I have been exceptionally skilful in choosing my allies or exceptionally fortunate in them, but I can declare unhesitatingly that I have never had a hard word with a collaborator while our work was in hand and never a bitter word with him afterward. My collaborators have always been my friends before and they have always remained my friends after. Sometimes our literary partnership was the unpremeditated outcome of a friendly chat in the course of which we chanced upon a subject, and in sport developed it until unexpectedly it seemed promising enough to be worthy of artistic consideration. Such a subject belonged to both of us, and had best be treated by both together. There was no dispute as to our respective shares in the result of our joint labors, because we could not ourselves even guess what each had done when both had been at work together. As Augier said in the preface to the 'Lionnes Pauvres,' which he wrote with Édouard Foussier, we must follow the example of "the married people who say one to the other, 'your son.'"

I have collaborated in writing stories, in making plays, and in editing books. Sometimes I may have thought that I did more than my share, and sometimes I knew that I did less than I should, but always there was harmony, and never did either of us seek to assert a mastery. However done, and by whichever of the two, the subject was always thoroughly discussed between us; it was turned over and over and upside down and inside out; it was considered from all possible points of view and in every stage of development. When a final choice was made of what seemed to us best, the mere putting on paper was wholly secondary. I have written a play of which I prepared the dialogue of one act and my associate prepared that of the next; I have written a play in which I wrote the scenes in which certain characters appeared and my ally wrote those in which certain other characters appeared; I have written a short-story in two chapters of which one was in my autograph and the other in my partner's: but none the less was he the half-author of the portions I set on paper, and none the less was I the half-author of the portions he set on paper.

Probably the most profitable method is that of alternate development; certainly it is for a drama. After the subject begins to take form, A makes out a tentative sequence of scenes; and this, after several talks, B fills up into an outline of the story. Slowly, and after careful consultation, A elaborates this into a detailed scenario in which every character is set forth, every entrance and every exit, with the reasons for them, every scene and every effect—in fact, everything except the words to be spoken. Then B takes this scenario, and from it he writes a first rough draft of the play itself, complete in dialogue and in "business." This rough draft A revises, and rewrites where need be. Then it goes to the copyist; and when the clean type-written manuscript returns both A and B go over it again and again, pointing and polishing, until each is satisfied with their labor in common. Perhaps the drama is the only form of literature in which so painstaking a process would be advantageous, or in which it would be advisable even; but of a play the structure can hardly be too careful or too precise, nor can the dialogue be too compact or too polished.

"I am no pickpurse of another's wit," as Sir Philip Sidney boasts, but I cannot forego the malign pleasure of quoting, in conclusion, Mr. Andrew Lang's insidious suggestion to "young men entering on the life of letters." He advises them "to find an ingenious and industrious and successful partner, stick to him, never quarrel with him, and do not survive him."

(1890)